I0887097

The Christ Mystery

Reflections on the Second Coming

Robert A. Powell

RUDOLF STEINER COLLEGE PRESS

Rudolf Steiner College Press
9200 Fair Oaks Boulevard
Fair Oaks, CA 95628
FAX 916-961-3032

ISBN 0-945803-39-7

Acknowledgments

With heartfelt gratitude to Charles Lawrie, editor of *Shoreline* and *CLAS News*, for his encouragement which led to the writing of the original articles, and for his kind permission for them to be published here in book form; also to Dianna Christenson for her gracious secretarial help, and to others who have assisted in the production of this book.

Many thanks also to Claude Julien for publishing this book, and to others who have contributed (often through conversation) to the evolution of its content. This content is more than "mere ideas" for me as author. It represents the fruit of extensive reflection upon the Mystery of the Second Coming and would not be offered here if I were not convinced of its truth. However, the reader must also carry his or her own responsibility to test this content for its objectivity, as a necessary step in the process of assimilating it.

Robert A. Powell

Contents

Foreword

On several occasions I have been asked if the series of articles I wrote for the journal *Shoreline* (1988-1992) on the Second Coming of Christ might be republished. The publication of this work, *The Christ Mystery*, is in response to this request and at the same time goes further. The first four chapters are, apart from minor alterations, identical with the four articles published in *Shoreline*. Then follows the article "Tribulation and the Second Coming" that was published in *CLAS News* No. 1 (1993). (*Shoreline* ceased publication in 1992, and *CLAS News* in 1993.) "Living in Apocalyptic Times" is the text of a lecture held in Boulder, Colorado, on August 2, 1996. And "Great Signs from Heaven" is an essay (hitherto unpublished) that brings my reflections on the Second Coming up to date—with, among other heavenly signs, the appearance of the comets Hyakutake and Hale-Bopp in 1996 and 1997. The Christ Mystery is concerned with the greatest mystery of our time: the Second Coming. It is intended as a contribution to help find an orientation to this event.

The event of Christ's Second Coming has ushered in a New Age. Today almost everyone has heard of the New Age, but few people realize that it has to do with Christ's Second Coming. And, as far as I know, Rudolf Steiner (1861-1925), the founder of Anthroposophy, was the first person to speak of the New Age. Again and again he referred to the start of the New Age in 1899. However, he did not say how this date is connected with the onset of Christ's Second Coming.

In my book *Chronicle of the Living Christ*[1] I have given a basis for understanding the commencement of the New Age in 1899. By way of analogy, this may be thought of as a "reincarnation" of Christ—however, not in a physical but in an etheric body. Two thousand years ago he incarnated in a physical body. Now he is "reincarnating" in an etheric body. And it is the rhythm of his etheric body that underlies this reincarnation. The rhythm of his etheric body is 33 1/3 years, this being the length of time from his birth on December 6, 2 B.C., to his resurrection on April 5, A.D. 33.

Normally, at the moment of death the etheric body separates from the physical body, leaving behind the latter as a corpse, and dissolves into the etheric cosmos. At the death and resurrection of Jesus Christ, however, the etheric body did not dissolve but remained intact. This etheric body contains all the memories of his life, extending back to birth. Thus the rhythm of Christ's etheric body corresponds to his biography of 33 1/3 years. As his etheric body did not dissolve back into the cosmos at the resurrection in A.D. 33, what then transpired?

The answer is that Christ, together with his etheric and astral bodies, ascended to the realm of the zodiac, this being the outer expression of the Kingdom of the Father. In his own words, spoken to Mary Magdalene on the morning of the resurrection: *"Do not touch me, for I have not yet ascended to the Father, to my God and your God"* (John 20:17). This ascent began forty days later on Ascension Day when he merged into a cloud of light upon the Mount of Olives, and two Angels appeared from the cloud of light and said to the disciples: *"Men of Galilee, why do you stand looking up to heaven? This Jesus, who was taken up from you into heaven, will come again in the same way as you saw him go into heaven"* (Acts 1:11). With this, the Angels proclaimed the return of Christ, his Second Coming. And it is the rhythm of 33 1/3 years that enables us to follow Christ's ascent and his return in 1899.

On this path of ascent, commencing in A.D. 33, Christ ascended through the ranks of the nine spiritual hierarchies: Angels, Archangels, Archai, Exusiai, Dynamis, Kyriotetes, Thrones, Cherubim, Seraphim, the passage through each hierarchy lasting 3 x 33 1/3 = 100 years. Thus the passage through the angelic hierarchy lasted from A.D. 33 to 133, that through the hierarchy of the Archangels from 133 to 233, and so on, until the passage through the Seraphim from 833 to 933. This is exactly the same path followed by the human soul in the life after death, as described by Rudolf Steiner and also by Dante in "Paradise," the third part of the *Divine Comedy*.

Having ascended through the nine spiritual hierarchies, Christ entered the realm of the fixed stars, the zodiac, the outermost expression of the Kingdom of the Father. Here the archetype of 33 1/3 years was relived and imprinted into the fixed-star world in the period 933-966. The year 966 represents the "midnight hour" of Christ's path of ascent and descent, the midpoint of his cosmic journey between 33 and 1899. In 966 the path of descent began, retracing in reverse the path of ascent, first living through again the archetype of 33 1/3 years from 966 to 999 before beginning the path of descent through the ranks of the nine spiritual hierarchies. Thus the period 999-1099 was that of the descent through the Seraphim, the period 1099-1199 that of his passage through the Cherubim, and so on until 1799-1899 as the period of Christ's descent in his etheric body through the angelic hierarchy (see figure on following page).

In 1899 there began the reintegration of Christ's etheric body into the etheric aura of the Earth, lasting 33 1/3 years until 1933. This signified the start of the New Age.

The Ascent of Christ through the Hierarchies and His Descent at the Second Coming

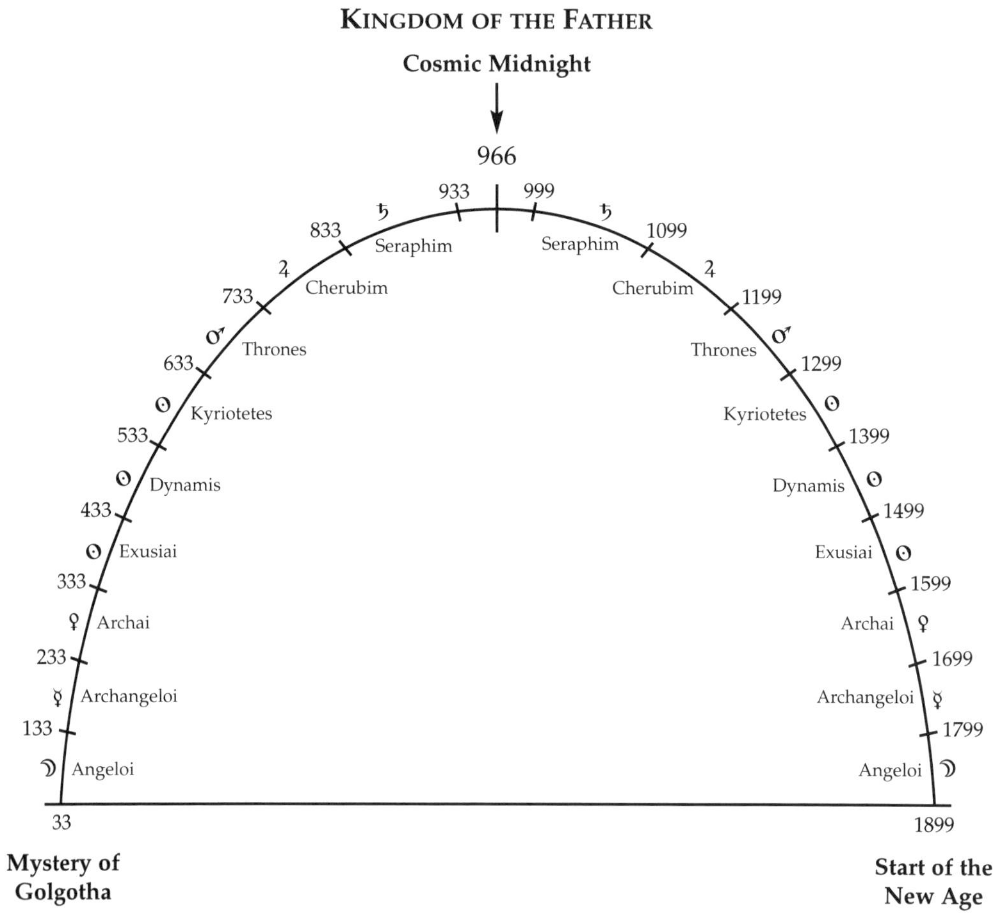

Christ's ascent and descent through the hierarchies was at the same time an ascent and descent through the planetary spheres. Christ's life was inscribed as an archetype into the world of the fixed stars from 933 to 966. The descent after the cosmic midnight (966) exactly mirrors the ascent.

Reflections on the Second Coming

The wave of Christ's etheric return repeats itself rhythmically every 33 1/3 years, mirroring his earthly life, and dividing each century into three parts. In this respect, the 33 1/3-year rhythm is a key rhythm underlying the New Age, the Age of the Second Coming. The first third of the twentieth century, during which the descent of the Risen One from cosmic heights was taking place, saw the birth of Anthroposophy in preparation for Christ's return to the etheric aura of the Earth. In Stockholm, on the evening of January 12, 1910, the founder of Anthroposophy, Rudolf Steiner, proclaimed the imminent return of the Risen One in etheric form to the Earth's aura. On this day in 1910 the Sun was in conjunction with the planet Uranus, the planet which is often associated with the bringing in of new impulses. Rudolf Steiner's deed at this moment of inspiration made him a prophet of the Second Coming—a kind of twentieth-century "John the Baptist"—but his death in 1925 precluded him from experiencing that which he had foretold: the completion of Christ's entrance into the Earth's etheric aura one-third of the way through this century, signifying the onset of the New Age.[2]

Acquaintanceship with Rudolf Steiner's lifework reveals that he was endowed with the faculty of being able to extend his consciousness not only to the Earth's etheric aura but also to cosmic realms beyond, within which he could behold the descent of the Risen One toward the Earth. Hence he could be certain of the truth of his proclamation concerning the Second Coming, even to the extent of dating the onset of this event to begin one-third of the way through this century. But for those whose consciousness has not yet developed to the extent of being able to perceive beyond the physical plane into the etheric world, the question remains: *Is it possible to know with certainty that the Second Coming within the Earth's etheric aura has already begun?*

Obviously there can be no "proof" of the Second Coming in the sense of a scientific demonstration, but nevertheless some evidence of this event has been provided by witnesses of the Second Coming who have reported their experiences. For example, there is the Russian witness of 1933 referred to in the appendix "The Second Coming" in my book *Hermetic Astrology*, Vol. I, who spoke of Christ beginning to move "from the west to the east in wavelike lines. He will begin in America and will continue through Europe to the northeast of Europe." Then again, there is the witness borne by David Spangler in his book *Revelation: The Birth of a New Age*: "Like most great events, the birth of the New Age occurred quietly . . . the Cosmic Christ descended and entered the life of Earth on all its levels . . . now Christ walks amongst us again, though clothed in etheric energy, and His Presence quickens the etheric and spiritual life of all who can open in love and peace, and responding, arise to His level . . . the true Second Coming has occurred and is this revelation and release of Christ Life within the inner planes of Earth . . . by Christmas 1967 the initiation was complete . . . the New Age had been born" (Chapter 4).

This can be interpreted to mean that the second 33 1/3-year period of Christ's etheric return within the Earth's etheric aura was completed by Christmas 1967 (actually in May 1966). Thus, although 1999 denotes the culmination of the third 33 1/3-year period measured from the cosmic commencement of the New Age in 1899, from the standpoint of the Earth and humankind, measured from the year 1933, the second 33 1/3-year period of the Second Coming culminates in the year 1999.

Apart from Rudolf Steiner, who was a herald of the New Age in its cosmic perspective, and who already in 1910 prophesied the onset of the Second Coming in the 1930s, apart from the witness of 1933 who described the beginning of the Second Coming within the Earth's etheric aura, and apart from David Spangler, who bore witness to the culmination of the first 33 1/3-year period since 1933—are there others who have experienced the Risen One in the twentieth century?

A remarkable book published in Stockholm in 1973 confirms the truth of Rudolf Steiner's prophecy, first made in that same city in the year 1910. Bearing in mind the words of the witness of 1933 concerning the Etheric Christ: "He will begin in America and will continue through Europe to the northeast of Europe," it seems not mere coincidence that a number of testimonies of experiences of the Risen One from people in Scandinavia have been recorded and presented in book form. It should be added that these testimonies, as far as can be judged, are from people who have no connection either with Anthroposophy or the "New Age" movement, people from all walks of life who have nothing in common apart from the Christian faith.

The book, entitled *They Experienced Christ*, was published as a report, compiled by Gunnar Hillerdal and Berndt Gustafsson, of the Religious-Sociological Institute of Stockholm. The first edition was published in Stockholm by Verbum in 1973 and a second edition in 1979. Also in 1979, a German translation, *Sie erlebten Christus*, translated from the Swedish by Dr. Boris Tullander, was published by Verlag die Pforte in Basel, Switzerland. The book's foreword implies that the book came about seemingly by chance. Some letters received by Gunnar Hillerdal, which reported unusual experiences ("meetings with Christ"), led Hillerdal, after consultation with Berndt Gustafsson, to place an advertisement in a large Swedish daily newspaper. This was on December 24, 1972. The response went far beyond the expectations of Hillerdal and Gustafsson. The wealth of reports they received, many deeply impressive and detailed descriptions of profound personal experiences, induced them to edit a selection of the accounts and present them in the form of a book.

Before considering the material published by Hillerdal and Gustafsson, it may be helpful to review some points made by Rudolf Steiner with respect to the Second Coming. On numerous occasions (from 1910 onwards) he spoke of the onset—in the course of the twentieth century—of a new "Christ revelation," the outcome of which would be such that a number of people would be able to perceive Christ in his etheric form. He called this the "greatest mystery of the twentieth century," but warned of dire consequences if it were not heeded by humankind. He emphasized that Christ would come in the etheric world, and would be active there for the good of humanity and the Earth, independently of whether or not he would be recognized by human beings. In his descriptions as to how people would experience the Etheric Christ, he pointed to him as a helper and comforter of needy, sick, and despairing human beings. Rudolf Steiner indicated how it would be possible for all human beings to draw near to Christ in what he characterized as the way to the Christ through thinking:

> Instead of taking an interest merely in my own way of thinking, and in what I consider right, I must develop a selfless interest in every opinion I encounter, however strongly I may hold it to be mistaken. The more someone prides himself on his own dogmatic opinions and is interested only in them, the further he removes himself, at this moment of world-evolution, from the Christ. The more he develops a social interest in the opinions of other people, even though he considers them erroneous, the more he does to fulfill in his inmost soul a saying of Christ, which today must be interpreted in the sense of the new Christ-language. Christ said: "Inasmuch as ye have done unto one of the least of these my brethren, ye have done unto me." The Christ never ceases to reveal Himself anew to human beings even unto the end of earthly time. And thus He speaks today to those willing to listen: "In whatever the least of your brethren thinks, you must recognize that I am thinking in him; and that I enter into your feeling, whenever you bring another's thought into relation with your own, and whenever you feel a fraternal interest for what is passing in another's soul. Whatever opinion, whatever outlook on life, you discover in the least of your brethren, therein you are seeking Myself." So does the Christ speak to our life of thought, the Christ who desires to reveal Himself in a new way—the time for it is drawing near—to the human beings of the twentieth century. . . . This is the way which today must be characterized as the way to the Christ through thinking (*The Inner Aspect of the Social Question*, pp.40-41).

Since experience of Christ in his Second Coming is on the whole an intimate subjective encounter with the Divine, most people who have had such an experience do not usually speak about it, except perhaps to their husbands or wives or close friends. For this reason these spiritual experiences, of a deep and profound nature, do not generally become communicated to a wider public. It is therefore something quite out of the ordinary that over one hundred people in Scandinavia reported their "Christ encounters" in writing, and that a selection of these reports has been published in book form. In a clear and remarkable way, these reports confirm Rudolf Steiner's prophetic announcement of the Second Coming.

Many of the appearances of Christ described in the book *They Experienced Christ* were to people in need, and to the sick. Of these, the following, related by a pregnant woman from Denmark who had become ill with malaria after visiting Thailand, gives an indication of the comforting presence of the Risen One to people in despair:

> On Christmas Eve my temperature soared rapidly again. I was brought to the maternity ward of the hospital, received painkillers, and came into a room where I was quite alone. The doctors and nurses encouraged me to be brave and not to be afraid. A nurse brought a bowl of red soup, and I ate it. Strange that I could do this. After the operation I was brought back to the room. A young doctor entered and said words to the effect that our child would not live. At these words everything went black, totally dark. Beyond time and space. Death. This I did not know. But suddenly He was there. I saw Him coming, but did not know who He was. With His left hand He took hold of my right and filled me with a joy that cannot be described with words; I felt blessedness, peace, joy, thankfulness. Words are unable to describe it.

A second account by a Norwegian woman relates her experience in a hospital after she had an accident in which her leg became bored through with steel wire. She lay in bed and suffered much pain. She said she felt herself abandoned by God. Then she heard someone coming. A figure drew near:

> He wore a long white garment, was tall and majestic, with a radiant golden crown on His head. In spite of the kingly appearance and sublime dignity, unending compassion streamed forth from Him. He said: "Today you have seen many doctors here, and you

> know that there is one who calls himself the head physician. You should know, however, that I am the one who is the head physician in this house, and this is my visiting time. When evening comes, when the lights are dimmed and the noise dies down, I make my rounds; for then I have a chance to speak to the hearts of those here. And I say to you: You thirst. I thirsted also; you feel yourself abandoned by God, so it was with me also; you have hard, cold iron in your flesh and blood, so had I also." He did not say more; He turned and disappeared. But I felt such joy that I could have leapt out of bed. . . . And I was allowed to feel in my own body something of that which He had suffered for all of us.

In this appearance the words of Christ from the cross are called to mind: *"I thirst"* and *"My God, my God, why hast thou forsaken me?"* as well as the fact of the hands and feet of Christ having been pierced through by nails.

Also frequently reported are appearances of Christ during holy communion, such as the following account, by a Swedish woman, of an experience she underwent in 1966 or 1967 in a church in Onsala:

> As the congregation went up to the altar to receive communion, I remained sitting. I thought I would not go alone today, but would wait for another occasion. I sat to the right in the church, one or two rows under the gallery. I believe that another person also sat beside me. As I was sitting and thinking this, I saw a brilliant appearance in the aisle, just in front of the row where I was sitting, approximately the height of a man. To my left I heard a voice which spoke the single word "Christ." It was as if someone was referring to this appearance in order to say who it was. A moment later I heard from this appearance the words: "Whoever does not eat and drink with me has no part of me." Then the whole appearance disappeared instantaneously. I do not know if this formulation is in the Bible, whether it was spoken by Jesus, but I recall the words exactly. I stood up immediately to go to the altar. . . .

In this appearance the words of Jesus Christ from the sixth chapter of the Gospel according to John are recalled: *"Truly, truly, I say to you, unless you eat the flesh of the Son of man and drink his blood, you have no life in you. . . . He who eats my flesh and drinks my blood abides in me, and I in him."*

Apart from appearances to the sick and needy, and apart from experiences in connection with holy communion, several artists report in *They Experienced Christ* of their encounters with Christ. One example is that of an artist who was painting a picture depicting Christ in the garden of Gethsemane:

> The whole time that I was painting the picture I regretted that I had agreed to sell it. When the painting was finished, I put it in front of the door to my balcony. I sat down on the sofa on the opposite side of the room. Then it seemed to me as if Christ's eyes and also His hands moved. The flowers in the garden began to come alive. They turned into human beings surrounding Christ. Then I saw Christ moving from one side of the painting to the other. Oh, how He spoke! But I recall only the word "Gethsemane." In a flash of lightning Christ disappeared, clothed in a light blue cloak. In his place sat Mary, clothed with a red cloak, and holding a baby in her arms. She moved and so did the child. A voice spoke, "Christ is born again." Then I saw again a flash of lightning and Christ stood there as before. He spoke the whole time; I saw how his lips moved, but now I heard no words. All this repeated itself several times. First it was Christ, then again Mary with the child.

Not all the encounters described in *They Experienced Christ* are of a visual nature. Several refer to the experience of the presence of Christ, a strong and unmistakable sensation of his nearness as a silent, comforting, guiding strength. Others describe inner auditory experiences of Christ in which words of help and consolation spoken by him are received quietly and inwardly. Almost all those who have had this latter kind of experience, as well as others who both saw him and heard him, convey their impression of his soft and gentle voice, full of love. Those who have seen him often describe the power of his loving gaze, his all-penetrating look. And many refer to the radiant light in which he is bathed, such as in the following account, also from the same book.

> Suddenly the room became indescribably full of light. It became so bright that the eyes hurt. The light radiated out from the middle of the room. An unparalleled radiance came from the lamp on the ceiling and spread forth in all possible kinds of beautiful rays, as if emitted by a star. In the midst of these rays stood Jesus, vibrantly alive, before me.

As far as it is possible to judge from the selection of reports in *They Experienced Christ*, a large proportion of the appearances of Christ took place at night, with midnight often being referred to. One account describes that it was the night of the Full Moon:

> It was a strange evening, Full Moon, and a tremendous storm. I stood at the window and looked at the clouds chasing across the heavens, and thought of a poem by Hjalmar Gullberg. After I had spoken the poem, someone came into my room. I knew instantly who it was, and sank upon my knees at the windowsill, and did not dare to turn my head to look at him. Light and peace radiated from him, transcending all understanding. I distinctly felt the touch of his hand as he bent towards me and took away my burden, the burden that I am not fit to be his servant. How long I knelt at the windowsill, I do not know. But outside, looking through the window, there appeared out of the dark cross [the shadow formed by the wood in the window] another cross, which was bright and reached up to heaven. His voice explained to me the mystery of the cross. I did not hear a voice, but the meaning of the cross became clear to me in a miraculous way. The whole question of sacrifice had been so difficult for me to grasp; now I suddenly understood, so I believe, the profound sense of Christ's deed and its significance for every single human being. A tremendously great perspective opened up. I saw the cross between heaven and earth as an axis about which everything revolves, the innermost mystery of creation . . . Divine Love.

This account calls to mind that Christ's death on the cross on Good Friday took place at the time of the Full Moon.

The foregoing descriptions translated from *They Experienced Christ* reveal that a number of people have had experiences of Jesus Christ in his Second Coming, since the onset of this event in the twentieth century. From these descriptions it is evident that Rudolf Steiner's prophecy is confirmed: appearances of the Etheric Christ can take place unexpectedly, anywhere, at any time, to anyone. Who can tell just how many people in our time may have had such experiences? Common to all these appearances is the experience of him as a comforter, helper, and source of healing strength. This profound, personal experience is unforgettable, a sacred memory, generally signifying not only a breakthrough to the religious dimension of existence, but also being accompanied by a great strengthening of the soul and of the life forces. To use Rudolf Steiner's words, this is the "greatest mystery of the twentieth century," betokening the arising of a New Age, an Age of Light.

Star Wisdom and the Holy Grail

Er jach, ez hiez ein dinc der grâl:
des namen las er sunder twâl
inme gestirne, wie der hiez.
'ein schar in ûf der erden liez:
diu fuor ûf über die sterne hôch.
(Wolfram von Eschenbach, *Parzival*, 454, 21-25)

He said there was a thing called the Grail
whose name he had read clearly
in the constellations.
A host of Angels left it on the Earth
and then flew away up over the stars.
(trans. H. Mustard and C. Passage, p. 244)

From the words quoted here it is evident that a cosmic mystery is connected with the Holy Grail, for reference is made to the stellar constellations and to a host of Angels. This angelic host bore the Grail, left it on the Earth, and then returned to the world of stars. How is this to be understood?

Legend connects the Holy Grail with the sacred vessel used by Jesus Christ at the Last Supper, and which at the crucifixion Joseph of Arimathea held under the cross in order to collect some of the Messiah's holy blood in it. The Grail thus bore the essence of Christ's Being, and symbolizes the mystery bound up with his blood, which became sacrificed for the redemption of the Earth and humanity. At the Last Supper the holy vessel bore the wine that Jesus Christ blessed and handed to his disciples, saying: "*Take the wine and share it among you; henceforth I shall drink no wine, until the Kingdom of God comes. Now a new era and a new sacrifice is beginning, which will last until the end of the world.*" According to legend, this was the same vessel with which Melchizedek instituted the sacrifice of bread and wine, which he handed over to Abraham, the founding father of the people of Israel. From Abraham the sacred vessel was handed down to Moses, and later it was part of the treasures of the temple, remaining in the temple until the time of Jesus Christ, when through divine dispensation, it became sold to one of his followers in Jerusalem.

Whatever the actual origins of the sacred vessel used at the Last Supper may be, it clearly symbolizes a mystery: the mystery of the covenant between God and humanity. The first covenant—at which Melchizedek played the role of mediator—was between God and the people of Israel, represented by Abraham; for Melchizedek, king of Salem, was priest of the Most High God. And the covenant instituted at the Last Supper was between the Son of God, Jesus Christ, and his followers, represented by the disciples. The covenant was brought to fulfillment at the crucifixion as the blood of Christ united with the Earth. This was the covenant, by way of Christ's blood, with the Earth itself. And it was the mystery of the eternal covenant with the Earth to which Joseph of Arimathea aspired, when he held up the sacred vessel to receive some of the blood as it issued forth from Christ's wounds. This mystery, however, has a cosmic dimension which could not be grasped by human beings at the time of Christ. For this reason the Mystery of Christ, symbolized by the Holy Grail, became preserved by Angels until the time became ripe for it to be revealed.

As the Grail legend recounts, Angels brought the Grail to Titurel, a mysterious and highly spiritual human being, who—like his predecessor Melchizedek in antiquity—instituted, in the service of the Most High God, the mystery of the communion from the Grail and founded the brotherhood of the Holy Grail. The Grail family descended from Titurel, and those called to serve the Holy Grail were able to grasp something of the Mystery of Christ more on the level of feelings, rather than in a fully conscious way. A more conscious participation in the Mystery of Christ was reserved for a later period of time, for the Age of the Second Coming of Christ.

There is an analogy between the communion instituted by Melchizedek, as preparation for the institution by Christ himself of the holy sacrament at the Last Supper, and the communion instituted by Titurel, as preparation for the more conscious participation in the mystery of the Holy Grail that is now becoming possible through the Second Coming of Christ. In the space of these pages only the briefest indications may be given concerning the Age of the Second Coming of Christ—the coming of Christ in his etheric body as a figure of light—the onset of which began earlier in this century, and which will last some 2500 years. (For the source of the ideas concerning the dating of the Second Coming, readers are referred to the appendix entitled "The Second Coming" in my book *Hermetic Astrology*, Vol. I, and also to the afterword of my book *Chronicle of the Living Christ.)*

Just as the Angels bore the Grail down from cosmic realms to Titurel, so with the onset of the Second Coming Christ himself descended from the cosmos toward Earth, passing through the sphere of Angels, cosmically the sphere bounded by the orbit of the Moon, between 1920 and 1932. After this came the onset of the Second Coming in the human realm, the earthly sphere, which may be dated to 1932/1933.

The period from 1920 to 1932 is of special significance, for during this time the Grail mystery became renewed within the angelic realm, not just on the level of feeling, but embracing human willing, feeling, thinking, and also the self of the human being. At the time of Titurel the possibility was opened up for those in the brotherhood of the Holy Grail to experience something of the Mystery of Christ on the level of feeling. This was enabled by way of the connection established between the angelic realm—in which this Mystery has been guarded since the time of Christ—and the human realm, beginning with Titurel. This was only a preparation, however, for the time when Christ himself would enter the angelic realm, when experience of the renewed Grail mystery would become more fully possible. This was during the period 1920 to 1932, during which a new connection between the angelic kingdom, i.e., the Moon sphere, and the human kingdom on Earth became opened up. But just as an individual worthy to fulfill the task of bearing the Grail mystery to human beings had to be found at the time of Titurel, so in the period following 1920 an individual was sought who would be worthy of bringing the new Grail impulse to humankind. This was Rudolf Steiner (1861-1925), founder of the Anthroposophical Society.

In fact, preparation for this task had begun in Rudolf Steiner's life already long before, parallel with the descent of Christ from cosmic realms. (As will be explained in the next chapter, this refers to the descent of the Christ Self, following a 12-year rhythm, which has to be distinguished from the 33 $^{1}/_{3}$-year rhythm of Christ's etheric body.) This descent may be followed with the help of a particular cosmic rhythm—the passage of Jupiter through the constellations of the zodiac. But in accordance with the cosmic nature of Christ, the Spirit of the Sun, it is the heliocentric orbit of Jupiter that is relevant. (Heliocentric means Sun-centered, signifying the orbits of the planets against a background of the starry constellations as seen from the Sun.) And the division of the constellations into unequal stellar groupings as in modern astronomy is not quite accurate; rather, it is the predecessor of the astronomical zodiac, the original astronomical/astrological zodiac of the Babylonians, Egyptians, and ancient Greeks—which is relevant here. This zodiac, known as the sidereal zodiac, comprises a division of the constellations into twelve equal stellar groupings, each 30° long, i.e., twelve sidereal signs in which the 30-degree sidereal signs coincide approximately with the constellations of the astronomical zodiac (see Figure):

Dates of the Sun's Ingresses into the Twelve Signs of the Sidereal Zodiac[3]

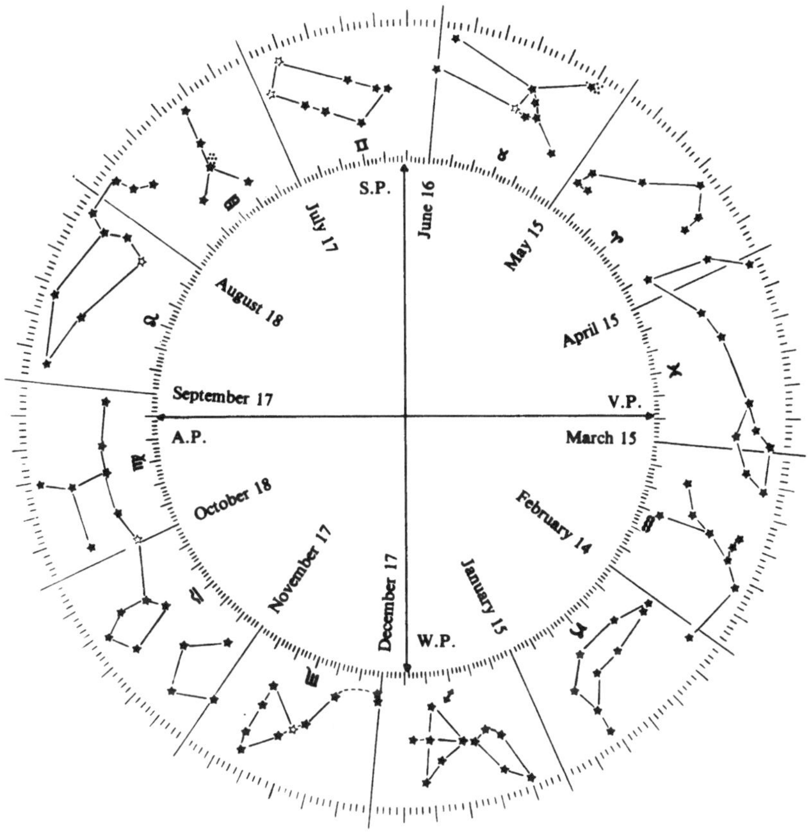

V.P. = vernal point = location of the Sun on (or around) March 21

S.P. = summer solstice point = location of the Sun on (or around) June 22

A.P. = autumnal point = location of the Sun on (or around) September 23

W.P. = winter solstice point = location of the Sun on (or around) December 22

In particular, it is the entrance (ingress) of Jupiter—viewed heliocentrically—into the sidereal sign of Leo that is the most important rhythm underlying the descent of Christ from cosmic realms toward Earth. This rhythm repeats itself every twelve years, less approximately seven weeks. The heliocentric ingress of Jupiter into sidereal Leo took place close to the summer solstice in 1920 and recurred again around Ascension Day in the year 1932. It was during this period that the passage of Christ through the angelic realm (Moon sphere) took place. Harmonizing with this rhythm of Jupiter, it emerges that the onset of the Second Coming—the reappearance of Christ in a spiritual form—in the human realm (the earthly sphere) coincided more or less with Ascension Day in 1932 (Thursday, May 5).

It was on Ascension Day in the year A.D. 33 (Thursday, May 14) that Jesus Christ departed from the earthly realm to begin his ascent to the cosmic realm of the Father, entering on the path of this ascent first of all into the angelic realm (Moon sphere), which borders the human realm. On this day the Christ, accompanied by his disciples, proceeded to the summit of the Mount of Olives, becoming ever more resplendent with light as he made his way. Upon reaching the summit, he shone with a light more radiant than the midday Sun. Then he raised his right hand and laid his left hand across his breast; turning slowly, he blessed the whole world. The glory of the light emanating from Jesus Christ became greater and greater until he disappeared into the cloud of light. From this light two Angels then appeared and addressed the apostles and disciples left behind on the Mount of Olives, saying in resounding tones: *"Men of Galilee, why do you stand looking up to heaven? This Jesus, who was taken up from you into heaven, will come in the same way as you saw him go into heaven."* The Angels then vanished into the receding cloud of light, returning to the angelic realm, the sphere bounded by the orbit of the Moon.

Just as Christ departed from the earthly realm in this way on Ascension Day A.D. 33, it emerges that his return—as promised by the Angels accompanying him—began some nineteen centuries later, around Ascension Day in the year 1932. This coincided fairly closely with the heliocentric ingress of Jupiter into sidereal Leo.

The modern quest for the Holy Grail is the search for the Risen Christ, who through his Second Coming has inaugurated a New Age. And a modern-day science of the Grail has the task of grasping the cosmic Mystery of Christ, which remained concealed to human beings (although sensed by some, such as Joseph of Arimathea) at the start of the Christian era, and only glimpses of which were possible to members of the brotherhood of the Holy Grail founded by Titurel in the eighth/ninth centuries after Christ. (Titurel was a contemporary of Charlemagne.)

A new star wisdom embodied in the new science of the Grail is concerned with, among other things, the mystery of communion, that is, the cosmic communion between humanity and the world of stars. Star wisdom, in the light of the Holy Grail, has the task of discerning when the cosmic configurations arise that are propitious for the inner communion of the human being with the Risen Christ. Such a configuration is indicated by Jupiter's heliocentric ingress into sidereal Leo. It was precisely this configuration that prevailed at Rudolf Steiner's birth on February 25, 1861 (see *Hermetic Astrology*, Vol. I, Chart 13, p. 220). This configuration repeated itself, at twelve-year intervals, on: January 1, 1873; November 11, 1884; September 21, 1896; August 4, 1908; June 15, 1920 and April 25, 1932. From Rudolf Steiner's birth until Michaelmas 1896, the descent of Christ from cosmic realms belonged to the Sun sphere, that of lofty spiritual beings (Kyriotetes, Dynamis, Exusiai) of the second hierarchy. On his path of descent through the Sun sphere, Christ was received into the realm of Kyriotetes without hindrance (1861-1873). But, during the passage (1873-1884) through the realm of the Dynamis he encountered resistance, which was mirrored on Earth in the Russo-Turkish war (1877-1878). The passage (1884-1896) through the realm of the Exusiai went unhindered, as also the descent (1896-1908) through the realm of the Archai, the Time Spirits.

It was in 1899, shortly after the entrance of Christ into the realm of the Archai, that Rudolf Steiner underwent a profound experience, a Christian initiation, which changed the whole course of his life and prepared him to become a spiritual teacher with the task of proclaiming the approach of the Second Coming. At this time of the start of the New Age, Christ was passing through the sphere of the Archai, and Rudolf Steiner later wrote in his autobiography (*The Course of My Life*) of this deep experience as having taken place toward the end of the nineteenth century. Through this experience in 1899 he became an apostle or prophet of the Etheric Christ.

The passage (1908-1920) of Christ through the sphere of the Archangels (Folk Spirits) called forth resistance, which became mirrored on Earth as World War I (1914-1918). Shortly after Christ's entrance into the cosmic sphere of the Archangels, Rudolf Steiner underwent an experience that enabled him to begin to proclaim with certainty that the Second Coming was underway and that soon some human beings would be able to behold the Etheric Christ in the earthly realm (as did the disciples between Easter and Ascension in A.D. 33). See, for example, the speech of Theodora in Rudolf Steiner's Mystery Drama *The Portal of Initiation*, which was first performed in Munich on August 15, 1910.

The passage (1920-1932) of Christ through the sphere of the Angels opened up a further new experience of the Second Coming for Rudolf Steiner. Out of this experience, he was called to inaugurate the Grail mystery anew in the twentieth century, the culmination of which took place on Christmas Day, 1923. At this Christmas Foundation Meeting of the Anthroposophical Society he was called—like Titurel more than one thousand years earlier—to renew the Grail Mystery, to establish a new connection between the human and angelic realms. The meditation revealed out of the angelic realm by Rudolf Steiner on this occasion—the Foundation Stone Meditation—refers to the sacred stone of love (a symbol for the Holy Grail), which embodies the Mystery of Christ (at that time descending through the angelic realm). The four verses of this meditation are directed in turn to human willing, feeling, thinking, and the self, to place them in connection with the cosmic ranks of the spiritual hierarchies and with the radiant Christ-Sun, who returns to humankind through the Second Coming, being born anew from the angelic realm into which he ascended on Ascension Day, A.D. 33.

A fully conscious experience of the content of this meditation is possible only from within the angelic realm from which it stems, where the Grail mystery is guarded—but the endeavor of the human being to bring this meditation to realization within constitutes a step in the direction of forming a new link between the human and angelic realms, toward a new participation in the Mystery of Christ.

The question remains: *What is the significance of the Jupiter rhythm referred to above, and why should it be connected with the descent of Christ through the cosmic spheres of the hierarchies toward the Earth?*

The heliocentric orbit of Jupiter denotes the boundary of the stage of cosmic evolution known as Ancient Sun (see Chapter 8 of my book *Hermetic Astrology*, Vol. II). It was during this stage of evolution that the etheric or life body of the human being was formed, and Christ's etheric body is essentially a body of life infinitely more intense than that of human beings. Christ's etheric body is, so to say, a "piece of Sun," and it accords with the rhythm of Jupiter carried over as a memory from Ancient Sun. This rhythm, viewed heliocentrically, is such that Jupiter requires almost twelve years to make one orbit of the sidereal zodiac, thus spending about one year in each zodiac sign. But why should the ingress of Jupiter into sidereal Leo signify the starting point of this rhythm (with respect to Christ), rather than, say, its entrance into sidereal Aries?

Here it is a matter of a mystery connected with the human heart, for the heart is formed out of the zodiacal forces emanating from sidereal Leo. And the heart—macrocosmically Leo—is the starting point for the development of the Christ impulse, which is implanted in the heart of every human being. Rudolf Steiner referred to the heart as the center into which the Foundation Stone of love is to become implanted in order to unfold its spiritual potential. The ingress of Jupiter, heliocentrically, into sidereal Leo corresponds macrocosmically to the unfolding of the new cycle of the Christ impulse, which may be taken up initially in the heart. In this light, the designation of Christ as the Lion of Judah—obviously referring to the zodiacal sign of Leo—is highly appropriate.

Lastly, looking at the dates of Jupiter's heliocentric ingress into sidereal Leo—its return to the same zodiacal location as at Rudolf Steiner's birth—we arrive at the following dates since 1932: March 12, 1944; January 22, 1956; December 3, 1967; and October 14, 1979. These dates are connected with the further passage of Christ since the onset of the Second Coming in 1932. In the period 1932-1944, when the Second Coming began in the earthly sphere, Christ's coming called forth a resistance in the human realm, and this became mirrored in World War II (1939-1945).

In each case the foregoing dates represent stages in the unfolding of the Christ impulse in the New Age, that of the Second Coming, which began in 1932. Only the briefest indications can be given here of the historical manifestations of the upsurge of new heart impulses mirroring this unfolding, each taking place as Jupiter was in sidereal Leo. In the social realm, the following were the most striking manifestations: in 1956 the popular uprising for freedom in Hungary; in 1968 the emergence in Czechoslovakia of "Socialism with a human face" (Prague Spring); in 1979/80 the arising of the Solidarity movement in Poland, calling for liberalization.

The date of the last heliocentric ingress of Jupiter into sidereal Leo was August 25, 1991, the time of the collapse of communism in the Soviet Union, following the failure of the coup (August 18-21) of hardline communists. All the above dates, although given exactly, should not be treated as exact to the day, for it is a matter of the unfolding of a cosmic impulse, which—like the growth of a plant—occurs gently. But these dates can be taken as indicators of stages along the way of the gentle process of the unfolding of the Christ impulse through the Second Coming. In this sense, contemplation of this Jupiter rhythm may contribute toward a new awareness of the cosmos and its rhythms, and of humanity's relationship to the cosmos in the quest of the Holy Grail, the search for a new and conscious communion with Christ, the cosmic communion, which the new star wisdom seeks to serve.

Sub-Nature and the Second Coming

In the foregoing I referred to the significance of Jupiter's orbit around the sidereal zodiac in connection with Christ's passage down from cosmic realms on his path of descent toward the Earth, prior to the onset of his Second Coming. And also I drew attention to the importance of the 33 1/3-year rhythm of Christ's earthly life for an understanding of the "wave" of the Second Coming.

In chapter 9 ("The Second Coming and the New Age") of my book *Hermetic Astrology*, Vol. II: *Astrological Biography*, I have expanded upon this and juxtaposed the two rhythms, giving exact dates. Summarizing the dates for the Jupiter rhythm:

Christ's Descent through the Hierarchies	**Planetary Sphere**	**Dates**
Kyriotetes - *Spirits of Wisdom*	Sun	Feb. 20, 1861 - Jan. 1, 1873
Dynamis - *Spirits of Motion*	Sun	Jan. 1, 1873 - Nov. 11, 1884
Exusiai - *Spirits of Form*	Sun	Nov. 11, 1884 - Sep. 21, 1896
Archai - *Spirits of Personality*	Venus	Sep. 21, 1896 - Aug. 4, 1908
Archangeloi - *Spirits of Fire*	Mercury	Aug. 4, 1908 - Jun. 15, 1920
Angeloi - *Spirits of Twilight*	Moon	Jun. 15, 1920 - Apr. 25, 1932

The dates given are those of Jupiter's heliocentric ingress (entrance) into sidereal Leo. These are the astronomically computed dates, and of course the actual dates of Christ's descent may differ somewhat from the computed dates. For example, the commencement of Christ's passage through the realm of the Kyriotetes coincided with Rudolf Steiner's birth on February 25, 1861, five days after Jupiter's heliocentric ingress into sidereal Leo.

With the completion of Christ's descent through the planetary spheres, there took place his entrance into the human sphere, in the earthly realm. The computed date is April 25, 1932, close to Ascension Day (May 5) in 1932. It was on Ascension Day (May 14) in A.D. 33 that Christ departed from the Earth to begin his ascension to the Father, when he took leave of the apostles and disciples on the Mount of Olives, to whom two Angels then proclaimed: *"Men of Galilee, why do you stand looking up to heaven? This Jesus, who was taken up from you into heaven, will come in the same way as you saw him go into heaven."* According to the foregoing, from one point of view it appears that the angelic proclamation of Christ's return, his Second Coming, can be dated approximately to Ascension Day, 1932. This is the date arrived at by following the Jupiter rhythm. However, a slightly different date is arrived at if we follow the 33 1/3-year rhythm of Christ's life. Let us now turn our attention to this second rhythm.

The time from the moment of birth of Jesus of Nazareth to the resurrection at dawn on Easter Sunday morning was exactly 33 1/3 years (less 1 3/4 days).[4] As will emerge in the following, this rhythm of 33 1/3 years is of immeasurable significance to the Earth and humankind, a rhythm that has repeated itself over and over again since the Mystery of Golgotha in A.D. 33.

For example, nine cycles of 33 1/3 years added to Easter Sunday (April 5) in A.D. 33 bring us to March 21, A.D. 333, which Rudolf Steiner often referred to as a critical turning point in human evolution. He said:

> Before the year 333 the greater part of the astral body had been active essentially in the upper man, and its smaller part in his lower body . . . . In the year 333 the two parts became equal. This was the critical situation 333 years after the coming of Christ, and since then the upper part of man's astral body has been continuously decreasing. That is the course taken by his evolution.[5]

Another crucial date frequently spoken of by Rudolf Steiner is 1899, the end of *Kali Yuga* (the Dark Age), which began—according to Hindu chronology—five thousand years previously, on February 17/18, 3102 B.C. (3102 B.C. = -3101, and 3101 + 1899 = 5000). Adding fifty-six cycles of

$33\,^1/_3$ to the date of the resurrection on April 5, A.D. 33, brings us to September 10, 1899. This coincided with the end of Kali Yuga and the start of the New Age, *Satya Yuga* (the Age of Light). As referred to in the foreword, the "reincarnation" of Christ in his etheric body, following the cosmic passage of ascent and descent between A.D. 33 and 1899 is the reason for referring to 1899 as the start of the New Age.

Thus, through coming to an understanding of the deeper significance of the $33\,^1/_3$-year rhythm, we are able to comprehend why it is justifiable to speak of the commencement of a New Age with the onset of the twentieth century. At the same time, we shall try to grasp the meaning of the 12-year Jupiter rhythm in relation to the $33\,^1/_3$-year rhythm. In order to take this step, however, it is helpful to seek to approach a deep and profound mystery concerning the relationship of Christ to the human being. This is one aspect of the Grail mystery, comprising the sublime mystery of the different modes of communion with Christ.

In order to approach this mystery we need the "magic wand of analogy" (to use Novalis's expression). The Hermetic principle of analogy offers us a key with which we may begin to grasp the relationship of Christ to the human being. Just as the human being is fourfold—comprising physical body, etheric body, astral body, and ego (or self)—so also it is possible for the human being to enter into a relationship with one or other of the members of Christ's being: his physical (or resurrection) body, his etheric body, his astral body, and his Self. This gives rise to four different kinds of communion with Christ. Let us consider these one by one.

The first mode of communion is that between the human self and Christ's Self. This is summarized in the words of St. Paul, *"Not I, but Christ in me."* This mode of communion is characterized by the fire of Christ's Love burning in the human being as a heightened power of spirit and an intensified awareness of the self and the world.

When, through the activity of the Christianized human self upon the astral body, the latter becomes purified and transformed, the ennobled astral body becomes capable of entering into communion with Christ's astral body. This second mode of communion is exemplified by St. Francis of Assisi, who, through his purified astral body, entered into an ongoing communion with Christ's astral body. This communion is characterized by mildness, gentleness, purity, and loving-kindness.

On the path of spiritual development it is possible not only for the astral body but also for the etheric body to become purified and transformed. This transformed etheric body then becomes capable of entering into communion with Christ's etheric body. St. Augustine provides us with an example of this third mode of communion, for, from a certain point in his life onward, he attained to a more or less ongoing communion with Christ's etheric body. This level of communion is characterized by a wonderfully harmonious and flowing quality of life and inner strength and creativity.

At a further stage of spiritual development the physical body itself undergoes a transformation, and here the possibility is opened up for the human being to enter into communion with Christ's physical (resurrection) body. It was this level of communion that the apostles experienced periodically during the forty days between the resurrection and the ascension, which filled them to the depths of their being and bestowed upon them new spiritual powers.

Just as we find the fourth mode of communion in the forty days following the resurrection, so we may also find the other three modes of communion revealed in the life of Christ. Thus, in the period from the death on the cross to the resurrection, it was the Self of Christ—alone, separated from the physical, etheric, and astral bodies—which descended into the underworld and then ascended again. In Christ's descent into hell, down to the *Kingdom of the Mother*, we find the archetype of the first kind of communion. Something of this search is found in the Grail legend of Parsifal, which also depicts the development of courage (on the part of the knights of the Grail), the courage needed to *descend into hell*, to meet with evil, to confront it and overcome it. Thus we find the first kind of communion as the central motif of the Grail legend of Parsifal. Parsifal may be considered as a representative of the *Jupiter human being*, who has brought to realization St. Paul's words, *"Not I, but Christ in me,"* and who has the courage to descend into hell, to take up the battle against evil for the sake of humankind and Mother Earth. The Jupiter human being is the human being of the future (Jupiter being the next stage of evolution after the Earth). And the planet Jupiter, with its 12-year rhythm, is of particular significance for those consciously endeavoring to take the path toward becoming Jupiter human beings, as well as for the first mode of communion—that between the human self and Christ's Self.

Returning to consider how the four kinds of communion reveal themselves in the life of Christ, so far we have found the archetype of the first mode of communion in the descent into hell and that of the fourth in the forty days leading up to the ascension. But where are we to find the archetypes of the other two modes of communion?

Here it is a matter of communion with Christ's etheric body and with his astral body. At the moment of death, when the human being separates from his physical body, leaving it behind as a corpse upon the Earth, he is then indwelling his etheric body. And inscribed into the etheric body are all the experiences he has undergone during the days of his life. Here the word "days" is appropriate, as the experiences undergone during sleep are not inscribed in the etheric body; rather, they are inscribed in the astral body, which the human being indwells during sleep, when the physical and etheric bodies are left behind in the sleeping condition. Thus, at the moment of death the human being, indwelling his etheric body, experiences a panorama of images of the experiences that he underwent during the course of life between birth and death, for these images are inscribed in the etheric body. Many people who have "died" (or been at the brink of death), and who have then returned to life, have described this experience of beholding a panoramic vision of all of life's experiences.

For our considerations the important point to note is that whereas the physical body belongs to the spatial realm, i.e., it exists in three-dimensional space, the etheric body belongs to the temporal realm, i.e., it is a *time body* in which the human biography is recorded. And at the moment of death the entire biography—from the moment of birth to the moment of death—is vividly experienced. The moment of death is actually a "birth," a birth into a higher realm. And the moment of the resurrection on Easter Sunday morning was also a moment of birth, the birth of the Risen One. The biography of the Risen One extended from the birth in Bethlehem to the moment of resurrection. Thus the etheric body of Christ contained all the experiences from the moment of birth in Bethlehem to the resurrection, comprising a time span of 33 $^1/_3$ years. But whereas at the death of the human being the etheric body, generally speaking, dissolves back into the cosmos, in the case of Christ his etheric body did not dissolve but has remained preserved. More than this, it has been—and continues to be—active, unfolding its activity every 33 $^1/_3$ years. Since the Mystery of Golgotha, therefore, the 33 $^1/_3$-year rhythm has played a role in the cosmic order, just as the planets always have done, e.g., Jupiter's 12-year rhythm and the 29 $^1/_2$-year rhythm of Saturn. In contrast to the planetary rhythms, which are specified in terms of cosmic space (that is, by their passage against the background of the zodiacal constellations, so that a planet's rhythm is determined by the time period that elapses between its conjunction with a given fixed star until its return to conjunction with the same fixed star), the 33 $^1/_3$-year rhythm is a purely temporal rhythm, specified by the duration of the life of Jesus Christ.

However, since the commencement of the New Age at the start of the twentieth century, the 33 $^1/_3$-year rhythm has begun to play a much more significant role than hitherto. This has to do with the Second Coming of Christ. For, whereas the First Coming was an event on the physical plane, the Second Coming is taking place on the etheric plane of existence, that is, in the realm of life forces. And it is especially Christ's etheric body that is active here.

As outlined in the foreword, following the Mystery of Golgotha in A.D. 33, the etheric body of Christ expanded slowly out into cosmic realms, attaining its greatest expansion in A.D. 966. This year denoted a point of transition. There then began a slow path of return of Christ's etheric body back toward the Earth. With the end of the fifty-sixth 33 $^1/_3$-year cycle on September 10, 1899, denoting the close of Kali Yuga, there began a reentry of Christ's etheric body into Earth's etheric aura; this attained a certain level of completion 33 $^1/_3$ years later, on January 8, 1933. Here the New Age—Satya Yuga (the Age of Light)—was born, whereby 1899 can be likened to the "dawn" and 1933 to the "sunrise" of the New Age. It was precisely during this period that Rudolf Steiner's teaching activity unfolded, from 1900 to 1925. Rudolf Steiner described Anthroposophy (spiritual science) as preparing the way for the Second

Coming, the approaching advent of which he repeatedly proclaimed from 1910 onward. Thus we see that Rudolf Steiner acted as a kind of "John the Baptist," proclaiming the approaching Second Coming, just as John the Baptist had prepared the way for the First Coming nineteen centuries previously.

At the First Coming the life of Jesus Christ lasted 33 1/3 years, of which the last 3 1/2 years—the ministry, from the baptism to the Mystery of Golgotha—were the most important. In contrast, the Second Coming is an event relating primarily to the etheric world and which, in accordance with the 33 1/3-year rhythm, will last for 2500 years, i.e., for seventy-five 33 1/3-year cycles, extending from September 10, 1899 to May 20, 4399. During these 2500 years the most important rhythm is the 33 1/3-year cycle of Christ's etheric body, and through a comprehension of this rhythm the possibility is given of attuning to this etheric body. It is the renewed presence of this etheric body in the Earth's etheric aura which has given birth to the New Age, thus opening up the possibility of a new communion (here described as the "third communion") with Christ.

What, then, is the relationship of the 12-year Jupiter rhythm (referred to earlier) to the 33 1/3-year rhythm, with respect to the Second Coming?

In order to be able to grasp this, we need to distinguish between the different members of Christ's being: Self, astral body, etheric body, and physical (resurrection) body. The central rhythm of the New Age is the 33 1/3-year rhythm of Christ's life, and the presence of his etheric body in the Earth's etheric aura is what has given birth to the New Age. However, if we were to take into consideration solely the 33 1/3-year rhythm, this would amount to looking at the renewed presence of Christ's etheric body in isolation from the other members of Christ's being. While acknowledging that Christ's etheric body is of central importance for the Second Coming, as this event is taking place in the etheric realm, we should not lose sight of the fact that all four members of Christ's being are united together and actively involved in the event of the Second Coming. And it is especially in relation to the Self of Christ that the 12-year Jupiter rhythm may be seen.

As mentioned earlier, the 12-year Jupiter rhythm is of significance with respect to the first mode of communion, i.e., communion with the

Self of Christ. The archetype underlying this communion is the *descent into hell,* which was undertaken by the Self of Christ following the death on the cross. And just as at the First Coming there was a descent and a reascent of the Self of Christ, so with the Second Coming there is again a descent and reascent taking place, however, over a considerable period of time.

At the start of this chapter the descent of Christ through the hierarchies from the Sun sphere down to the Earth is dated in connection with the 12-year Jupiter rhythm—from Rudolf Steiner's birth in 1861 up to Ascension Day in 1932. This gives us insight into the cosmic phase of the descent of Christ's Self in his Second Coming. But this cosmic phase of descent was only the prelude for the next stage of descent, which again can be followed in connection with the 12-year Jupiter rhythm.

With the heliocentric ingress of Jupiter into sidereal Leo around Ascension Day 1932, there began the passage of Christ's Self through the earthly sphere, the sphere of humankind. Resistance arose to his Second Coming, the opposition finding its central focus in the figure of the *Führer,* who tried to set up a Third Reich, a kingdom of evil, opposed to the kingdom of heaven. The ensuing struggle resulted in the Second World War (1939-1945). By Easter 1945 the Allies had effectively won the war in Europe, and a decisive step in the war with Japan was the Hiroshima bomb on August 6, 1945. By this time a new 12-year Jupiter cycle had commenced, and Christ's descent into the underworld—the sub-earthly realms—had begun. However, in order to understand this new phase in Christ's descent, it is helpful to look back to the archetype of this event at the Mystery of Golgotha.

On Good Friday, April 3, A.D. 33, shortly after carrying the cross up Mt. Calvary—it was about midday that he arrived at the summit, Golgotha—Jesus was stripped of his clothes and was then nailed to the cross. At 12:30 P.M., just as the trumpets sounded across from the temple to announce the slaying of the Passover lambs, the cross was raised up and the crucifixion began. At this moment in time, east of Jerusalem, the sidereal sign of Leo started to rise across the horizon (1° Leo). Here began the slaying of Christ, the Lion of Judah. The crucifixion lasted during the rising of Leo, and as the death on the cross took place the sidereal sign of Virgo had just begun to rise. At the moment of death, at 3 P.M., the

Ascendant was 2 1/2° Virgo (all degrees in terms of the sidereal zodiac). There then took place a mighty earthquake, rending the earth in two at the foot of the cross, and the radiant Spirit of Christ—Christ's Self—descended down from the cross into the bowels of the Earth. Here commenced the fulfillment of the *sign of Jonah* prophesied by Christ: *"For as Jonah was three days and three nights in the belly of the whale, so will the Son of man be three days and three nights in the heart of the earth"* (Matt. 12:40). The "three days and three nights" spoken of here are not to be taken literally—for the descent and reascent lasted only thirty hours—but we may imagine that thirty hours in the underworld ("hell") could be spoken of allegorically as "three days and three nights in the heart of the Earth."

For our considerations it is of significance that Christ's descent into hell began with the rising of Virgo. For the deeper meaning of Christ's descent to the heart of Earth was to reunite with the Mother, prior to his ascent to the Father. And, as the sign of Virgo corresponds to the womb in the female organism, so it was appropriate—in terms of cosmic symbolism—that the descent of Christ into the womb of Mother Earth began as Virgo started to rise.

Knowledge of the deeper significance of Christ's descent into hell as being a descent into the underworld to reunite with the Mother belongs to the Grail mysteries. And it is this mystery of the descent to the Mother that is central to Christ's Second Coming. Just as at the Mystery of Golgotha the descent began with the rising of sidereal Virgo, so with the Second Coming the descent into the underworld began with Jupiter's heliocentric ingress into sidereal Virgo, during the Easter night (Saturday/Sunday), March 31/April 1, 1945. And just as the earthquake at the foot of the cross was the outer sign of Christ's descent into hell at the Mystery of Golgotha, so the opening up of the Earth's interior through the Hiroshima bomb on August 6, 1945, was an outer sign of Christ's descent at the Second Coming—albeit this time a man-made sign inspired by an evil force of destruction working up from the underworld. By August 6, 1945, Jupiter heliocentrically had already reached 9 1/2° Virgo; however, geocentrically Jupiter was at 2 1/2° Virgo, coinciding with the zodiacal degree rising at the time of Christ's death on the cross. The spiritual event of the commencement (at Easter 1945) of Christ's descent into the underworld—indicated by Jupiter's heliocentric ingress into sidereal Virgo—became proclaimed on the physical plane by the explosion of an atomic bomb at Hiroshima, coinciding with Jupiter geocentrically reaching 2 $1/2°$ Virgo. With this explosion there began the atomic age, which, spiritually understood, is the age of confrontation with the forces belonging to the underworld.

In order to arrive at a deeper understanding of the time in which we live, it is helpful to look more closely at the stages of the descent of Christ's Self into the underworld, starting in 1945. Again it is the 12-year Jupiter rhythm that is important here. But whereas the stages of cosmic descent (1861-1932) through the realms of the spiritual hierarchies are connected with Jupiter's heliocentric ingress into sidereal Leo, the stages of the descent into hell are related to Jupiter's heliocentric ingress into sidereal Virgo, starting in 1945. In between, during the period from Ascension Day 1932 to Easter 1945, was a time when Christ's Self was present in the earthly sphere of humanity—a time of suffering on the part of Christ comparable to his Passion of Good Friday in A.D. 33. Indeed, World War II (1939-1945) was a kind of *second crucifixion* of Christ (preceding his second descent into hell)—a crucifixion on the etheric plane of existence, within Earth's etheric aura.

In order to be able to comprehend Christ's descent into the underworld, we need to know something of its structure. According to Rudolf Steiner, nine sub-earthly spheres may be distinguished, leading down to the heart of the Earth.[6] These nine sub-earthly spheres may be thought of as mirroring the nine cosmic spheres of the nine spiritual hierarchies. And just as each sphere of the spiritual hierarchies contains a particular kind of goodness (the love of the Seraphim, the harmony of the Cherubim, and so on), so each sub-earthly sphere is the source of a particular kind of evil. The evil of each sub-earthly sphere is the inverse of the goodness belonging to the corresponding cosmic sphere. For example, over and against the love of the Seraphim belonging to the highest cosmic sphere is pitted the hatred for Christ stemming from the deepest sub-earthly sphere, that is, the ninth. And against the harmony of the Cherubim is the divisive influence of the eighth sub-earthly sphere, which is the source of all strife and disharmony.

The earthly sphere of humanity, in which the human being normally spends his waking existence between birth and death, is placed between the nine cosmic spheres of the spiritual hierarchies above, extending up to the Kingdom of the Father, and the nine sub-earthly spheres of the powers of evil below, which are situated in the interior of the Earth, inserted between humankind and the Kingdom of the Mother. Every human being incarnated upon the Earth is subject to the interplay of forces that work into him both from the heavens above and from the realms below. Generally speaking, what works up from below is of a subconscious nature, and the forces of evil working from the nine sub-earthly spheres into the human being's subconscious have to be overcome—a first step being to become conscious of these evil forces. However, not everything that works up from below is evil, for also that which belongs to the Kingdom of the Mother works into the human being from below. How may we begin to understand the Kingdom of the Mother?

As a starting point, let us consider Rudolf Steiner's words from the night of the Full Moon, April 5/6, 1909, which he chose for the laying of the Foundation Stone of the Rosicrucian temple at Malsch, near Karlsruhe, Germany:

> We want to sink the foundation stone of this temple into the womb of our Mother Earth, beneath the rays of the Full Moon shining down upon us here, surrounded by the greenness of nature enveloping the building. And just as the Moon reflects the bright light of the Sun, so do we seek to mirror the light of the divine-spiritual beings. Full of trust we turn towards our great Mother Earth, who bears us and protects us so lovingly. . . . In pain and suffering our Mother Earth has become hardened. It is our mission to spiritualize her again, to redeem her, in that through the power of our hands we reshape her to become a spirit-filled work of art. May this stone be a first foundation stone for the redemption and transformation of our Planet Earth, and may the power of this stone multiply itself a thousandfold.[7]

Here it is significant that the night of the Full Moon was chosen for the laying of this foundation stone, for the Moon became full also on the evening of Good Friday in A.D. 33 when Christ began his descent into the womb of the Earth, down to the Mother. Rudolf Steiner also described the color seen clairvoyantly arising from the depths, from the Kingdom of the Mother:

> The silver-sparkling blue below, arising from the depths of the Earth and bound up with human weakness and error, is gathered into a picture of the Earth Mother. Whether she is called Demeter or Mary, the picture is of the Earth Mother. So it is that in directing our gaze downwards, we cannot do otherwise than bring together in Imagination all those secrets of the depths which go to make up the material Mother of all existence. While in all that which is concentrated in the flowing from above, we feel and experience the Spirit Father of everything around us. And now we behold the outcome of the working together of the Spirit Father with the Earth Mother, bearing so beautifully within itself the harmony of the earthly silver and the gold of the heights. Between the Father and the Mother we behold the Son.[8]

Since the time of ancient Greece, following the rise of Christianity, knowledge of the Mother and the "secret of the depths" has more or less disappeared from human consciousness. The cult of Demeter celebrated in the Eleusinian mysteries at Eleusis was suppressed by the Emperor Theodosius at the end of the fourth century A.D. But now, in the twentieth century, through the Second Coming of Christ, a new access to the Earth Mother and her mysteries is opening up. It would lead too far afield to go into details here, but summarizing briefly, there is a threefold mystery connected with the Mother:

> that of the Name of the Mother (known to the Greeks as Demeter);
> that of her Kingdom (known in the Orient as Shamballa);
> that of her Will (eternal faithfulness to the Father, despite the fact, since the Fall, of the Mother's withdrawal into the darkness of the underworld).

Concerning the lost Kingdom of the Mother, it is interesting to consider Rudolf Steiner's words to Countess Johanna von Keyserlingk at the end of the *Agricultural Course* (Whitsun/Pentecost 1924) at which he laid the foundations for a new and conscious relationship to Demeter through a spiritually based agriculture (bio-dynamic farming):

> Rudolf Steiner was good enough to come up to my room, where he spoke with me about the Kingdom in the interior of the Earth. We know that at the moment Christ's blood flowed onto the Earth a new Sun-globe was born in the Earth's interior. My search had always been to penetrate the depths of the Earth, for I had seen raying up from there an Earth-core of gold, which Ptolemy designated as the "Archetypal Sun." I could not do otherwise, again and again, than to bring this golden ground into connection with the land of Shamballa, of which Rudolf Steiner had spoken. He had recounted how this land had disappeared from the sight of human beings and that Christ would open the door to those human beings seeking it, to lead them to the "sunken, fairy-tale land of Shamballa" of which the Hindus dream. . . . I asked Rudolf Steiner, "Is the interior of the Earth of gold, originating from the empty space within the Sun, actually belonging back there again?" He replied, "Yes, the interior of the Earth is of gold." For the sake of certainty, I asked him further, "Herr doctor, if I stand here upon the ground, then beneath me, deep in the interior of the Earth, is the golden land. If I were to attain to freedom from sin and were to remain standing in the depths, the demons would not be me and I would be able to pass through them to the golden land. Is this so?" He replied, "If one passes through them together with Christ, then the demons are unable to harm one, but otherwise they would be able to destroy one!" He added the significant words, "However, they are able to become our helpers. Yes, this is so. The path is right, but it is very difficult!"[9]

Here, therefore, we see that the path to the Mother is beset with difficulty owing to the nine *spheres of evil* inserted between humanity and the Kingdom of the Mother, but that together with Christ this path is possible. As referred to earlier, this path has become opened up to humanity at large since 1945.[10] Previously it was accessible only to the highest initiates. But, at the same time, with the *opening of the gates of hell* humanity has become increasingly exposed to the demonic influence of the sub-earthly spheres.

Against this background certain developments in the twentieth century may be viewed. And, as outlined above, the only safe way in which we can begin to look at these developments is together with Christ. Thus, it is in connection with the descent of Christ himself, in his Second Coming, that we shall now briefly review the course of the twentieth century. But before taking this step, we can find help in knowing that the nine Beatitudes spoken by Christ at the Sermon on the Mount contain the Christian impulses to counteract the demonic influences of each of the nine sub-earthly spheres. For example, the sixth Beatitude is: *"Blessed are the pure in heart, for they shall see God."* This "purity of heart" counteracts the demonic influence of the sixth sub-earthly sphere, which is the source of evil passions that, if they were to take hold of a human being, would render him oblivious of the spiritual world and make him conscious only of his lower impulses, leading to utter depravity. The nine Beatitudes, therefore, are of key significance on the path of accompanying Christ on his descent into hell. Further, it should be remembered—since the human being is a microcosm reflecting the macrocosm—that the nine sub-earthly spheres are also within each human being, and that the descent into hell is at the same time a descent into one's own being. In fact, each of the nine Beatitudes refers to a particular member of the human being, and correspondingly the nine sub-earthly spheres are the source of counter-impulses to the nine members of the human being.

Supplementing the table at the beginning of this chapter, we can add to the passage of Christ through the spheres of the spiritual hierarchies, culminating in his passage through the spheres of the Archangels (1908-1920) and of the Angels (1920-1932), the passage through the realm of humanity between Ascension Day 1932 and Easter 1945. Then follows Christ's descent into the underworld, where also the relationship underlying the counterimpulses to the nine members of the human being is indicated, as follows:

Christ's Descent through Sub-Earthly Spheres:	Source of Counter-impulses to:	Dates:
1. Mineral Earth	physical body	Apr. 1, 1945-May 20, 1933
2. Fluid Earth	etheric body	Apr. 1, 1945-Feb. 10, 1957
3. Air Earth	astral body	Feb. 10, 1957-Dec. 21, 1968
4. Form Earth	sentient soul	Dec. 21, 1968-Nov. 1, 1980
5. Fruit Earth	intellectual soul	Nov. 1, 1980-Sep. 11, 1992
6. Fire Earth	consciousness soul	Sep. 11, 1992-Jul. 23, 2004
7. Earth Mirror	spirit self (manas)	Jul. 23, 2004-Jun. 3, 2016
8. Earth Severer*	life spirit (buddhi)	Jun. 3, 2016-Apr. 14, 2028
9. Earth Core	spirit man (atma)	Apr. 14, 2028-Feb. 24, 2040

**The eighth sub-earthly sphere is also known as the Divisive Layer.*

The dates given are those of Jupiter's heliocentric ingress into sidereal Virgo, and these astronomically computed dates may differ somewhat from the actual dates of Christ's descent. On this path of descent, it is a matter in each sphere of a confrontation with a particular kind of evil. We can begin to gain a comprehension of this struggle by way of analogy with the confrontation that took place in the human realm on Earth between 1933 and 1945. The powers of evil working from the sub-earthly spheres found a vehicle in the human kingdom ("the Führer") to act as a focus of their opposition to the Second Coming. Through this vehicle a full-scale attack was launched, which was the counterpart to the impulse brought by Christ. This counterimpulse can be followed down to the last detail. For example, instead of *"Hallowed be thy name,"* the chant arose on Earth to hallow ("heil") the name of the Führer. And instead of *"Thy kingdom come"* the Führer sought to establish an evil kingdom (the Third Reich) in place of the Kingdom of God.

A titanic struggle ensued, resulting in World War II, which can be regarded as a *second crucifixion*, as referred to earlier. However, with the triumph over evil in 1945, the conflict was not ended. Although 1945 signified the end of conflict in the human realm on Earth, the confrontation went on to continue in the sub-earthly spheres, into which Christ descended, signifying the opening of the gates of hell. The explosion of an atomic bomb at Hiroshima (and then at Nagasaki) was a man-made sign of the *opening of the gates of hell*, whereby the Earth's surface—which may be likened to an eggshell (enclosing the Earth's interior, comprising the sub-earthly spheres and the Kingdom of the Mother)—became shattered. Through the Hiroshima bomb the first major crack appeared in the "eggshell" separating the Earth's surface from the underworld ("hell"). Actually, the first crack appeared already on July 16, 1945, with the first test explosion of an atomic bomb at Alamogordo Air Base near Albuquerque, New Mexico.

In fact, this "eggshell" is itself the first sub-earthly sphere, the Mineral Earth. As such, it is not really a sphere like the other eight sub-earthly spheres, but a layer separating the human realm from the underworld. Already during the period preceding 1945, especially during World War II, the influence of the Mineral Earth was exerting an ever stronger hold on human consciousness. In 1939/1940 work began in Britain and the U.S.A. on the search for the military application of nuclear fission. This led, under the direction of Enrico Fermi, to the first self-sustaining nuclear chain reaction, which took place in Chicago on December 2, 1942. This whole line of scientific research was symptomatic of the increasing influence of the Mineral Earth upon human beings. How may the influence of this first realm of sub-nature be described?

Here an approach to the sub-earthly spheres may be found through the Beatitudes, which contain the counterimpulses to the sub-earthly spheres. For the first sub-earthly sphere, the Mineral Earth, the first Beatitude is relevant: *"Blessed are the seekers of the spirit, for theirs is the kingdom of heaven."* The influence of the Mineral Earth is the opposite of this impulse, leading to a turning away from the spirit, turning toward the earthly kingdom—the mineral, material, mechanical realm and its laws. The line of scientific research that led to the explosion of the Hiroshima bomb is an example of this turning, starting with the disintegration of the nuclei of lithium through bombardment by artificially generated protons, first carried out by John Cockcroft and Ernest Walton at the Cavendish Laboratory, Cambridge, on April 13, 1932. Then, on September 12, 1933, Leo Szilard had the idea of a nuclear chain reaction, which subsequently became realized in Chicago in 1942 as part of the "Manhattan Project," through the collaboration of Leo Szilard with Enrico Fermi and others.

The whole direction of scientific research, under the sway of the spirit-denying influence of the Mineral Earth, was characteristic of the first Jupiter period—that preceding 1945—of the Age of the Second Coming. This was a period during which a counterimpulse to that connected with the physical body held sway. Indeed, the titanic struggle that took place during World War II was a struggle for dominion of the kingdom (Reich) on the physical plane of existence and for the very existence—physically—of countless human beings. This meant that the first Jupiter period of the Age of the Second Coming was one in which, instead of the impulse of seeking for the spirit, for the kingdom of heaven, there lived the counterimpulse of turning away from the spirit to the earthly kingdom, especially the kingdom of matter.

In the second Jupiter period (1945-1957), coinciding with the descent of Christ through the second sub-earthly sphere (Fluid Earth), a new counterimpulse began to play into humankind's life on Earth. How may this be characterized?

The relevant Beatitude is, *"Blessed are those who bear suffering, for they shall be comforted."* The counterimpulse belonging to the Fluid Earth is one of caring only for oneself, avoiding suffering, according to the principle of the "survival of the fittest." In the wake of the devastation, pain, and suffering caused by World War II, there was ample opportunity for a new consciousness to awaken worldwide among humanity—one of caring and sharing, give and take, comforting the mourning ones. But with the crack in the "eggshell"—the rupture in the Mineral Earth—caused by the entrance into the atomic age, something quite new entered in and began to play a role in human life on Earth. What was this?

Here arose the counterimpulse to the etheric body. The etheric body is a subtle body of life forces interpenetrating the physical body. At the separation of the etheric body from the physical body at the moment of death the true nature of the latter is revealed in the shape of the corpse. The etheric body is the bearer of the principle of life, and the counterimpulse to this is *anti-life*. This is the substance of the Fluid Earth, the second sub-earthly sphere, and with the cracking of the Mineral Earth through the atomic bomb, massive quantities of this anti-life substance were released on Earth in the form of radioactive fallout. The quality of radioactivity is that it is life-destroying. As soon as it is brought into connection with anything living, it destroys this life.

Against the background of Christ's passage through the second sub-earthly sphere, the development from 1945 onward may be seen. In each sub-earthly sphere a confrontation with the evil at work in that sphere takes place—a confrontation that depends, in the first place, on becoming conscious of the nature of the evil principle at work. Thus many people became inspired, after World War II, to take up the challenge offered by the confrontation going on here. For example, Leo Szilard took up the crusade, as a leading atomic scientist, of bringing to consciousness the fearful implications of atomic war. In 1947 he formed the Emergency Committee of Atomic Scientists with Albert Einstein as chairman, and he also initiated the movement for the civilian control of atomic energy. Later, in Washington, he organized the Council for a Livable World.[11]

Nevertheless, the governments of the United States and the Soviet Union continued to support the line of research that led to the Hiroshima bomb. Consequently, on March 1, 1954, the United States exploded a hydrogen bomb on Eniwetak Atoll, Marshall Islands, in the Pacific, reckoned to be six hundred times more powerful than the Hiroshima bomb. In the wake of this explosion 287 people within a radius of 160 miles of Eniwetak Atoll suffered from the radioactive fallout. Most strongly affected were a group of twenty-three Japanese fishermen less than forty miles from the site of the explosion, who were covered with ash raining down from the atmosphere. One of them died within a few days, and the others all became marked with the incurable consequences of radioactive contamination. Radioactive fallout was measured around the globe, even as far away as Heidelberg in Germany. Following suit, on November 22, 1955, the Soviet Union exploded a still more powerful hydrogen bomb in the atmosphere above Siberia. With these two hydrogen bomb explosions the arms race took a sinister turn of development, and further major cracks were caused in the Mineral Earth, allowing the anti-life substance of the Fluid Earth to find its way in large quantities—via radioactive fallout—onto the Earth's surface.

Thus, after the attack on the level of the physical body signified by World War II, came the attack on the etheric body, in which radioactive fallout is the principle bearer of the anti-life principle belonging to the second sub-earthly sphere. However, the attack on the etheric body also began to make itself noticeable in other ways—the main hallmark being the interpenetration of the etheric body with electrical effects through increasing use of electrical household goods, and also the spread of television, in the postwar years. Another potent means toward the "electrification" of the etheric body that surfaced in this period was the advent of rock 'n' roll, which broke through to public consciousness in 1956. With this occurrence, however, preparation was made for a new onslaught, arising from the third sub-earthly sphere, the Air Earth.

Along the path of Christ's descent into hell, his passage through the Air Earth took place in the years from 1957 to 1968. The Christ principle active during this time is to be found in the third Beatitude, *"Blessed are the meek, for they shall inherit the Earth."* This relates to the human astral body, to the Christianizing of the astral body through meekness or, expressing it more actively, through loving-kindness, goodness, and peace. The counterimpulse from the Air Earth works to paralyze the astral body, to cut it off from cosmic astrality, whereby the suffocating atmosphere of the third sub-earthly sphere has the effect of annulling feeling.

Just as the Hiroshima bomb was a man-made sign of the cracking of the Mineral Earth, opening up contact with the Fluid Earth, so there was a man-made sign of the opening up of a connection with the Air Earth. This was the launching of the first Sputnik by the Soviet Union on October 4, 1957—an artificial satellite that encircled the Earth above the Earth's atmosphere. With this step the space age began. The deeper significance of this step was the beginning of cutting humanity off from cosmic-spiritual realms of existence by way of inserting man-made constructions—satellites, rockets, and space stations—between the cosmos and the Earth. This on the macrocosmic level corresponds to the effect on the microcosmic level of the Air Earth in cutting off the human astral body from cosmic astrality.

Following the example of the Soviet Union, on February 1, 1958, the United States made its first successful launching of a satellite into space to encircle the Earth above the Earth's atmosphere. Then, on April 12, 1961, Yuri Gagarin orbited around the Earth in a spaceship. This feat was matched shortly after by the United States when, on February 20, 1962,

John Glenn encircled the Earth in a space capsule. After this the United States emerged triumphant in the space race, accomplishing the remarkable feat on July 21, 1969, of landing two men on the Moon.

It is in adolescence that the astral body comes to the fore in the development of the human being—this being a time of awakening of sexuality and the feeling life, also often a time of turbulent emotions. In the period under consideration (1957-1968), because of the confrontation that arose in the third sub-earthly sphere on account of Christ's passage through this realm, there took place an onslaught of evil directed at the astral body. Moreover, there were many signs of a kind of *cultural adolescence.* One of the main signs was the rise and spread of pop (rock) music. As already mentioned, this broke through with significant force already in 1956, toward the end of the previous Jupiter period. In this connection reference was made to the negative effect of electrified music on the etheric body. But in addition it also has a detrimental effect upon human emotions and thus upon the astral body, in the sense of the counterimpulse of the Air Earth. Pop music, on the whole, works on the level of the adolescent feeling life. The phenomenal spread of pop music during the period under consideration points to the onslaught of evil, from the third sub-earthly sphere, directed at the astral body. Whereas genuine music (Bach, Mozart, Beethoven, and others)—being a reflection of the harmonies of the spheres—is capable of elevating the astral body toward cosmic-spiritual realms, the effect of pop music, generally speaking, is to set up a connection between the astral body and the third sub-earthly sphere, thus dragging the astral body down.

The astral body was formed in the preceding cosmic aeon, the Moon period of existence, and so the astral body has a strong relationship to the Moon. The United States' space mission, which initially had as its primary goal the landing of human beings on the Moon, unfolded by and large during the Jupiter period under consideration (1957-1968), motivated in part by the subconscious relationship to the Moon. In fact, at the completion of this Jupiter period, on December 21, 1968, the United States launched Apollo VIII, which orbited around the Moon ten times. This was followed, shortly after the start of the next Jupiter period, by the launching on July 16, 1969, of Apollo XI, which carried Neil Armstrong and Edwin Aldrin to land on the Moon. This latter event denoted—in an inverse sense—a kind of "coming of age" of humanity, following the period of cultural adolescence. We shall return to this below, after considering some further aspects of the Jupiter period from 1957 to 1968.

The Moon forces in the human being come to expression most directly in sexuality, the awakening to which generally takes place during adolescence. During the period of cultural adolescence from 1957 to 1968 this awakening came to expression in the shape of the "sexual revolution" which then took place. At the same time, with the introduction and subsequent widespread use of the contraceptive pill, a further step was taken in cutting off humanity from its divine origins. This can be understood quite simply from the fact that conception is—and always has been—the door through which incarnating souls enter on their path of incarnation into a physical body on Earth, and therefore the deliberate and systematic prevention of conception acts as a closing of this door to the realm of souls.

At the same time an onslaught was launched, by way of books, films, and magazines, to corrupt and pervert every aspect of sexuality, to desecrate its holy and sacramental character. In this connection the words of Hermes addressed to Asclepius (Greek text written prior to the end of the third century A.D.) are relevant:

> In the conjunction of the two sexes, or, to speak more truly, that fusion of them into one, which may be rightly named Eros, or Aphrodite, or both at once, there is a deeper meaning than man can comprehend. It is a truth to be accepted as sure and evident above all other truths, that by God, the Master of all generative power, has been devised and bestowed upon all creatures this sacrament of eternal reproduction, with all the affection, all the joy and gladness, all the yearning and the heavenly love that are inherent in its being. And there were need that I should tell you of the compelling force with which this sacrament binds man and woman together, were it not that each one of us, if he directs his thought upon himself, can learn it from his innermost feeling. For if you note that supreme moment when, through interaction without pause, we come at last to this, that either sex infuses itself into the other, the one giving forth its issue, and the other eagerly tak-

> ing hold of it and laying it up within, you will find that at that moment, through the intermingling of the two natures, the female acquires masculine vigor, and the male is relaxed in feminine languor. And so this sacramental act, sweet as it is, if it were done openly, the ignorant should mock, and thereby the deity manifested in either sex through the mingling of male and female should be put to blush—and the more so, if the act is exposed to the eyes of impious men.[12]

Through exposure, therefore, as effected by way of the media, the divine aspect of sexuality is driven out. But over and above this, the rise and spread of pornography has served not only to debase sexuality but also to pervert and corrupt it. This, too, is connected with the counterimpulse upon the astral body working from the third sub-earthly sphere, the Air Earth.

Yet another aspect of this counterimpulse manifested itself during the period under consideration in the drug epidemic—the widespread use especially of hallucinogenic drugs such as marijuana, hashish, mescaline, and LSD—which spread in this Jupiter period. It was above all this counterimpulse that corrupted the true impulse—that of the third Beatitude: *"Blessed are the meek, for they shall inherit the Earth"*—which was seeking to come forth at that time. The impulse of love, peace, and brotherhood ("flower power") that arose at that time was a genuine inspiration of the Christ impulse at work in the transformation of the astral body. However, through the drug prophets such as Timothy Leary, whose experiments with LSD date from the late '50s, a counterimpulse became directed at the astral body. For the activity of the Christ impulse in transforming the astral body leads to the development of conscious clairvoyance (*Imagination*), this being a metamorphosis of the dream consciousness of the astral body. On the other hand, the use of hallucinogenic drugs serves to call forth an artificially induced atavistic clairvoyance in which the dream consciousness of the astral body is activated without the conscious *participation* of the human self, thus leading to hallucinations instead of Imaginations. Therefore hallucinogenic drugs may be seen directly in relation to the counterimpulse of the third sub-earthly sphere upon the astral body.

These are just some of the phenomena that can be seen in connection with the confrontation between the Christ impulse and the counterimpulse of the Air Earth in the period from 1957 to 1968. There are other phenomena as well, but here it is not possible to go into too many details. Briefly, though, the following two phenomena may be mentioned:

(1) The fight against racial discrimination, from the days of Little Rock, Arkansas, in September 1957 to the shooting on April 4, 1968, of Dr. Martin Luther King, Jr., whose martyrdom did much to help the cause of establishing racial equality. Just one week later, on April 11, 1968, under Lyndon B. Johnson the Civil Rights Law was passed, which (from a legal standpoint) essentially ended racial discrimination in the United States.

(2) Student rebellion, which reached a climax in Europe, particularly in France, in May 1968, in the mass demonstrations and ensuing clashes with the police, resulting in the closure of the Sorbonne.

After this, as mentioned earlier, a kind of "coming of age" took place on a cultural level. The student rebellion that reached a climax in 1968 was the last phase of the period of cultural adolescence that came to an end in December 1968. The man-made sign of the new phase that opened up in 1969 was the landing of human beings on the Moon, referred to already. This extraordinary feat symbolized the birth of the human being as a *citizen of the cosmos*, albeit as a caricature of what is meant in a spiritual sense by these words. Here again a counterimpulse was at work. For the human being's true destiny is to become a citizen of the cosmos in a spiritual sense, through an awakening of consciousness to include the cosmic dimension of existence. And the physical landing on the Moon worked to counter this awakening by influencing human consciousness toward an awareness directed solely to the physical-material dimension of the cosmos.

Following upon the Moon landing, the United States' space program went on to begin to explore the solar system, sending off rockets to Mars and Jupiter. Mariner 9 encircled Mars on November 13, 1971, and Pioneer 10 passed close by Jupiter on December 4, 1973. The space program serves to intensify a physical-material conception of the cosmos, leading to a completely false impression of the human being's relationship to the cosmic-spiritual world. This can be seen in relation to the counterimpulse of the fourth sub-earthly sphere, the Form Earth. In this sphere forms become inverted and caricatured. And the space program has helped to build a kind of *"negative image"* of the solar system. This negative image is devoid of all spirituality and completely excludes the human being, except as a spaceman. However, the human being viewed as a spaceman, encapsulated in his space suit, is a negative image of the spiritual human being who is bound up with the whole cosmos. The entrance into the era of space travel, opened up by the Moon landing in 1969, can thus be viewed directly in connection with the counterimpulse of the fourth sub-earthly sphere.

In terms of the *opening of the gates of hell* occasioned by Christ's descent through the sub-earthly spheres, the period from 1969 to 1980 is that of confrontation with the evil of the fourth sub-earthly sphere, directed against the sentient soul of the human being. The true impulse for this period, connected with the fourth stage of the unfolding of the new Christ impulse in the Age of the Second Coming, is conveyed by the fourth Beatitude: *"Blessed are those who hunger and thirst after righteousness, for they shall be filled."* Something of this impulse inspired those who demonstrated for peace, especially for peace in Vietnam, who hungered and thirsted for a righteous solution to the unjust situation there. On November 13/14, 1969, some 250,000 demonstrators for peace gathered in Washington, the largest demonstration of its kind ever to have taken place there.

However, the influence of the fourth sub-earthly sphere is to turn everything into its negative. And the "hunger and thirst for righteousness" in its negative form can give rise to terrorism. It is against this background that the escalation of violence in Northern Ireland may be seen, which began with the wave of unrest that broke out there in August 1969, resulting in the sending of British troops to Ulster. The relationship between the Catholics and Protestants of Northern Ireland is something on the level of the sentient soul, beneath the reasoning level of the intellectual soul, and thus seems to defy the rational intellect. Here the counterimpulse directed against the sentient soul began to work in 1969. The influence of this counterimpulse is to render the human being insensitive to the just claims of his fellowmen, so that he becomes infatuated with his own claims for justice, and everything else seems to him to be wrong and unjust. It is this that fans the flames of terrorism.

Not just in Northern Ireland, but also elsewhere, terrorism raised its ugly head during the period under consideration. In February 1970 Arabs and Palestinians—again people living mainly on the level of the sentient soul—launched several terrorist attacks. Later, on September 5, 1972, Arab terrorists at the Olympic games in Munich killed two Israeli sportsmen and took nine hostages, all of whom were killed in the attempt by police to free them. Also in 1972 the Baader-Meinhof terrorist gang in Germany carried out attacks in May, prior to the capture of Andreas Baader on June 2, 1972. Murder, kidnapping, and bombing became widespread as a consequence of terrorist activity, one of the worst examples—toward the close of this Jupiter period—being the bombing of a railway station in Bologna on August 2, 1980, by a right-wing terrorist group, in which 83 people died.

On the positive side may be mentioned the increase in the movement for human rights during the 1970s, Amnesty International being the best-known example. Thus, in January 1977 "Charter '77" was issued in Prague, signed by more than 250 prominent people, calling for liberalization there. Twelve years later one of the signatories—the playwright Vaclav Havel—became President of Czechoslovakia, after having been persecuted and imprisoned as a result of his call for democracy. Here we see the triumph of the hunger and thirst for righteousness! Another example of the positive manifestation of the Christ impulse in this period became evident in the work of Mother Teresa in caring for the sick and needy people of Calcutta. In recognition of her work, on December 10, 1979, Mother Teresa received the Nobel prize for peace.

On the whole, however, it was the counterimpulse that came to the fore in the period from 1969 to 1980. This was the Brezhnev era in which the cold war grew in intensity, characterized by Brezhnev's inverted sense of justice: "When forces hostile to socialism seek to reverse the development of any socialist country whatsoever . . . this becomes the concern of all socialist countries." What this Brezhnev doctrine really signified was the claim on the part of the Soviet Union to the right to provide "military aid to a fraternal country" (meaning the right to invade) whenever there was a "threat to the common interest of the camp of socialism" (meaning a challenge to Soviet dominance). Reading between the lines, the inverting influence of the Form Earth can be clearly seen, producing a negative image of true righteousness, which in the case of the Soviet Union would mean allowing the people of each land to determine the future of their own country.

In the United States a negative image of righteousness emerged in the Watergate scandal involving the attempted bugging of the Democratic headquarters in Washington by five members of the Committee for Reelection of the President (the president being Richard Nixon). Through his attitude with regard to the Watergate affair, and in the face of a persistent search for the truth on the part of some investigators, Nixon was eventually obliged to resign as president.

In the cultural realm, alongside the increase in violence and terrorism, a more positive development was the opening up on a widespread level of interest in esoteric and spiritual matters. The New Age movement quickly gained momentum, a key step in this development being the publication of David Spangler's *Revelation: The Birth of a New Age* by the Findhorn Foundation in 1971. Whereas David Spangler, a major prophet of the New Age movement, is essentially Christian, most New Age impulses arose out of an Eastern influence: for example, yoga, tai ji quan, breathing exercises, meditation practices, and various forms of healing—many of these being directed primarily to the sentient soul and thus demanding little intellectual endeavor or deeper consciousness.

One disturbing phenomenon of the period under consideration is the massive increase in drug addiction, especially addiction to heroin. As referred to earlier, the hallucinogenic drugs, which enjoyed such widespread popularity during the 1960s, are directed at the astral body and to the dreamlike picture consciousness connected therewith. Heroin, which is injected into the blood, the bearer of the self, directly attacks on the level of the soul, the sentient soul. It overwhelms the human feeling nature and works in the sense of the fourth sub-earthly sphere by making the human being insensitive to virtually everything outside the immediate sense of his own well-being.

On November 1, 1980, a new Jupiter period began, which lasted until 1992. Just three days into this period, on November 4, 1980, Ronald

Reagan became president of the United States. The Reagan era began. At the same time a new phase in Christ's descent into the underworld commenced, this confrontation being with the evil belonging to the fifth sub-earthly sphere, the Fruit Earth. A sign of this new stage of confrontation with evil emerged in the shape of the AIDS virus, which attacks the life-support system of the human being. And the people who are most subject to this virus are those who seek the exuberant energy of egotistically directed life forces. Exuberant energy is the characteristic of the substance of the Fruit Earth.

The drug most related to this quality of the Fruit Earth, the fifth sub-earthly sphere, is cocaine. And as the fifth sub-earthly sphere bears the counterimpulse to the intellectual soul, so cocaine is directed against the intellectual soul, just as heroin is directed against the sentient soul. Both heroin and cocaine work into the blood, the bearer of the self, which they attack. But whereas heroin overwhelms the feeling nature (sentient soul), cocaine overwhelms the mental nature (intellectual soul). In the confrontation with the counterimpulse to the intellectual soul, which began in 1980, it is not surprising that addiction to cocaine has taken on epidemic proportions. Through cocaine's ability to stimulate a relationship with the exuberant energy of the Fruit Earth, the cocaine addict establishes an inner connection with this fifth sub-earthly sphere, just as the heroin addict does with the fourth sub-earthly sphere, and the hallucinogenic drug user with the third sub-earthly sphere. Seen in this light, drugs are instruments for demonic beings from the underworld to gain access to the human soul or astral body. The war against drugs is actually a war against demonic forces and beings that take possession of human beings and drag them down inwardly in the direction of the sub-earthly spheres.

The redeeming impulse to these demonic forces is the Christ impulse. And it is the fifth Beatitude that indicates the nature of the Christ impulse relevant here as the positive impulse countering the evil belonging to the fifth sub-earthly sphere: *"Blessed are the merciful, for they shall receive mercy."* Here it is a matter of compassion and forgiveness, not of making intellectual judgments. When Ronald Reagan branded the Soviet Union as an "evil empire," he passed judgment on a whole people. Unfortunately, he allowed his over-hasty judgment to form the basis of his armaments policy, which led to a massive buildup of nuclear arms and the commitment to SDI (also called "Star Wars" in the media), a fantastically expensive defense project to defend the United States against the "evil empire." All of this is a far cry from the merciful attitude implicit in the fifth Beatitude. In fact, SDI, if it were to have become realized, would have represented a further step along the path of cutting off the Earth and humankind from the spiritual cosmos.

When Mikhail Gorbachev became party chief of the Soviet Union on March 11, 1985, he could have had every reason to reciprocate Reagan's hostile attitude, in which case the cold war would have escalated further. But Gorbachev appears to have been imbued with the quality of mercy of the fifth Beatitude. He did not judge, but he came—in a spirit of openness—to meet Ronald Reagan. Similarly, later he came quite open-mindedly to meet George Bush. And, astonishingly for the head of an officially atheistic state, he came to meet Pope John Paul II in November 1989. On the day prior to his meeting the pope in Rome, Gorbachev said: *"We need a revolution of the mind."* Here it is evidently an impulse on the mental level (intellectual soul) that characterized Gorbachev's reforms, the key words of which were *glasnost* (openness) and *perestroika* (restructuring).

The spectacular achievement of Gorbachev's reforming impulse was to open up the possibility of democracy in the various Eastern European countries that, since 1945, were mere satellites of the Soviet Union. If we recall that democracy was born in Ancient Greece in the age of the development of the intellectual soul, it is easy to see on what level Gorbachev's reforming impulse was working and to see—at least, on its positive side—that it worked in conjunction with the Christ impulse. The deeper background to this is the preparing of the ground in Eastern Europe for the unfolding of a new culture there, one in which the Christ impulse will be able to emerge on a new level during the future Age of Aquarius.

The counterimpulse to the fifth Beatitude is cruelty and lack of mercy, which has its source in the fifth sub-earthly sphere. It was this impulse that took the upper hand among those in power in China, when the order was given that led to the massacre of hundreds of peacefully demonstrating students in Tiananmen Square during the early morning hours of June 4, 1989.[13] Again, seven years earlier, cruelty underlay the massacre of over one thousand Palestinian refugees on September 18, 1982, at the hands of Christian militia who entered the refugee camp in Beirut, while the occupying Israeli troops stood by and watched. It was mainly women, children, and old people who died under the hail of bullets. We may also think of the assassination attempts on Ronald Reagan, on March 30, 1981, and on Pope John Paul II on May 13, 1981, as symptomatic of the same counterimpulse. And the violence to which cocaine addicts are prone may also be mentioned in this connection.

This counterimpulse lives itself out in the thousands of murders and acts of violence that take place each year around the world, this being a major problem, especially in the larger cities. But in more subtle ways, too, this counterimpulse comes to expression, without necessarily being directly lived out. We need only think of the violence depicted in films and on television. More sinister, however, are the "video nasties" that depict savage and sadistic acts of violence and brutality, and thereby help to establish a link between human consciousness and the fifth sub-earthly sphere—just as pop music helps to facilitate a link with the third sub-earthly sphere.

Another modern phenomenon that in some cases tends to form an alliance between human consciousness and the counterimpulse directed against the intellectual soul is the computer, and especially in the past few years there has been a remarkable spread of home computers. While we cannot deny the beneficial aspect of computers, when rightly applied, an excessive preoccupation with them tends to one-sidedly overemphasize the intellect in a particular way, namely in the direction of a mechanical mode of thought. It is this mechanical element in the intellect that then forms a link with the sub-earthly spheres, in particular with the fifth sub-earthly sphere, which is the bearer of the counterimpulse to the intellectual soul. For the true nature of the intellectual soul, as may be seen by looking back to the Graeco-Roman period (the age of development of the intellectual soul), especially to the Greek philosophers, is *organic thinking*, which is at home in pondering the relationships between God, humanity, and nature. Organic thinking may be schooled by contemplation of the living, organic realm of nature. But in the case of an excessive preoccupation with computers, thinking becomes schooled by the machine and its rigid, inorganic logic; thinking becomes mechanized. From this simple consideration we can see that the mechanization of thought, which is an inherent danger for those who are obliged to deal extensively with computers in daily life, may be safeguarded against by purposefully cultivating living (organic) thinking.

Here attention may be drawn to the major role played by computers in the armaments race. Indeed, a project such as SDI would be unthinkable without the application of computers. As remarked upon earlier, the armaments race is built upon the opposite principle to that which is expressed in the fifth Beatitude, *"Blessed are the merciful . . . ."* And the SDI project, conceived of not long after the start of the 1980-1992 Jupiter period, epitomized a definite lack of the quality of mercy. The SDI project was a significant stage in the man-made signs of humankind's newfound alliance with sub-nature, with the sub-earthly spheres. The stages in this development, viewed in relation to the 12-year Jupiter rhythm are: the Hiroshima bomb (1945), the Sputnik launching (1957), the Moon landing (1969), and SDI, which was first announced publicly in 1983, but which may have been conceived of one or two years earlier. Apart from Sputnik (it was not until 1958 that the United States launched its own version, the Explorer satellite), each of these stages was an initiative on the part of the United States. It is in the United States of America, therefore, that the most powerful links between humanity and sub-nature have been evident. And this applies not just to the technological side of humanity's alliance with the sub-earthly spheres, but also to the cultural side.

The impulse living in the souls of the American people may be characterized by that which is termed the *descent into hell*. This, however, signifies confrontation with the evil of the sub-earthly spheres. And it is solely together with Christ that this descent may be accomplished in safety. This is the path to the Mother, Demeter, a path that in a somewhat different form existed in antiquity—for example, in the mysteries of Eleusis. To take this path means to begin to awaken to Mother Earth as a living being. And the worldwide awakening to environmental problems—the entire "Green Movement"—is indicative of the arising of a new consciousness of Mother Earth. In 1983 the Green Party was voted into the German parliament on a platform of protection of the environment, disarmament, and rejection of atomic energy. And there are signs that in the United States, too, politicians have begun to take environmental issues seriously. What a step it could have been if, instead of spending the proposed one trillion dollars on SDI (the estimated cost), that money could have been channeled into helping to solve environmental problems! Even though the Star Wars project was ultimately scrapped, the U.S. and other national governments still have a distance to travel in awakening to the virtue of mercy rather than that of raw power. Of both forces Shakespeare wrote:

> The quality of mercy is not strain'd,
> It droppeth as the gentle rain from heaven
> Upon the place beneath: it is twice bless'd;
> It blesses him that gives and him that takes:
> 'Tis mightiest in the mightiest; it becomes
> The throned monarch better than his crown;
> His sceptre shows the force of temporal power,
> The attribute to awe and majesty,
> Wherein doth sit the dread and fear of kings!
> But mercy is above the sceptred sway,
> It is enthroned in the hearts of kings,
> It is an attribute to God himself,
> And earthly power doth then show likest God's
> When mercy seasons justice.[14]

Just as the quality of mercy was central to the unfolding of the Christ impulse in the previous Jupiter period (1980-1992), so in the present period (1992-2004) it is the quality of purity: *"Blessed are the pure in heart, for they shall see God."* The sixth Beatitude relates to the new stage of unfolding of the Christ impulse, in the confrontation with the evil of the sixth sub-earthly sphere, the Fire Earth. Here, the counterimpulse to the consciousness soul is active. Instead of awakening human consciousness to the spirit (*consciousness soul*), the Fire Earth is a sphere of passion that fans aflame human passions, rendering the human being conscious of his lower nature and oblivious to his higher nature. He who becomes subject to the influence of the sixth sub-earthly sphere then receives his impulses from below, consisting of evil passions, and eventually may become utterly depraved. This is the counterimpulse to purity. Let us consider

Rudolf Steiner's words concerning the link between human passions and the Fire Earth:

> There are occasions when the very substance of the passions of the Fire Earth begins to rebel. Aroused by men's passions, it penetrates through the Fruit Earth, forces its way through the channels in the upper layers and even flows up into and violently shakes the solid Earth. The result is an earthquake. If this passion from the Fire Earth thrusts up some of the Earth's substance, a volcano erupts. . . . There is still this connection between human passions and the passion-layer in the interior of the Earth; and it is still to an accumulation of evil passions and forces that earthquakes and volcanic eruptions are due.[15]

Here is not the place to make predictions concerning the end of the twentieth century. It suffices to say that with the new level of working of the Christ impulse in the confrontation with evil—in the present Jupiter period (1992-2004)—the possibility is opened up of attaining a new and conscious relationship to the Christ impulse and to Christ's descent into hell. With the opening of the gates of hell along Christ's path of descent, at each stage a new level of the Christ impulse begins to unfold and at the same time a new, evil counterimpulse has to be met. The question could be raised: What is the point of it all? Why do we have to be confronted with the evil of the sub-earthly spheres?

The answer, quite simply, is that it is through the confrontation with and overcoming of evil that human beings are able to advance on their path of spiritual development—not just as individuals, but also humanity and the entire Earth. The forces of evil in the sub-earthly spheres are there whether we like it or not, and they work continuously into the human being on a subconscious level. The task is to raise them to consciousness, to recognize them for what they are, and to overcome them through the Christ impulse. The Christ impulse of purity (*"pure in heart"*) will help those who open themselves to it in the struggle with the awakening of bestial and depraved passions. In overcoming, human evolution advances a step further. In the words of Rudolf Steiner:

> You will see that human beings are related to all the layers [of the sub-earthly spheres], for they are continually radiating out their

> forces. Humanity lives under the influence of these layers and has to overcome their powers. When human beings have learnt to radiate life on Earth and have trained their breathing so that it promotes life, they will have overcome the Fire Earth. When spiritually they overcome pain through serenity, they overcome the Air Earth. When concord reigns, the "Divisive Layer" is conquered. When white magic triumphs, no evil remains on Earth. Human evolution thus implies a transformation of the Earth's interior.[16]

From this point of view, the present historical period—since the onset of the Second Coming—offers an unprecedented possibility for human evolution, through the confrontation with the evil of the sub-earthly spheres—a confrontation led by Christ, with Christ at our side. At the same time it is a period fraught with terrible danger, for never before in the history of humankind have the gates of hell been opened. And the positive advances seem small and frail in comparison with the onslaught of evil arising from the underworld through the *opening of the gates of hell.*

In the previous chapter some of the positive manifestations of the working of the Christ impulse in the twentieth century were mentioned: the popular uprising in Hungary for freedom (1956); the emergence in Czechoslovakia of "Socialism with a human face" (1968); the arising of the Solidarity movement in Poland calling for liberalization (1979/80). There reference was made to the fact that these events took place in connection with Jupiter's heliocentric passage through sidereal Leo. Looked at in relation to the unfolding of the Jupiter rhythm against the background of Christ's descent through the sub-earthly spheres, the passage through sidereal Leo always denotes the last phase of descent through a particular sub-earthly sphere. That is, when Jupiter is passing through sidereal Leo, the Christ impulse has—from one point of view—"triumphed" in the confrontation with evil in the sphere in question. The last heliocentric passage of Jupiter through sidereal Leo lasted from August 25, 1991, to September 11, 1992, which was the time of the "triumph" of the Christ impulse in the confrontation with the evil of the fifth sub-earthly sphere. This was the time of the collapse of the Soviet Union and the restructuring of the former communist countries of Eastern Europe.

Without going into too much detail concerning the further course of Christ's descent into hell, at the close of this chapter it is appropriate to give a brief summary. As indicated earlier, the deepest point on this path of descent will be attained in the year 2040, actually with the heliocentric passage of Jupiter through sidereal Leo from January 31, 2039, to February 24, 2040. Then Christ's reascent through the sub-earthly spheres will begin, which again may be followed in relation to the 12-year Jupiter rhythm. The descent, the passage through the "eggshell" of the Mineral Earth, began toward the end of the first Jupiter period of the Age of the Second Coming and was completed by about Easter 1945. The return through this "eggshell" will occur around the time of Jupiter's passage through sidereal Leo during the year 2134. This date falls close in time to the commencement of a new 33 1/3-year period on January 2, 2133.

As will be recalled, the 33 1/3-year rhythm is that of Christ's etheric body and is the key rhythm underlying the Second Coming. Thus, around 2133/2134 there will be a reunion of Christ's Self with his etheric body, an event analogous in importance to the resurrection on Easter Sunday morning in A.D. 33. There will then begin a period, which I have described in Appendix II ("The Second Coming") of *Hermetic Astrology I* as the core period of the Age of the Second Coming. There I dated this core period from 2133 to 4233, comprising three 700-year periods. This core period is analogous to the 40-day period in A.D. 33 that followed the resurrection and culminated with the ascension.

Thus the 200-year period from 1933 to 2133 (leading up to the core period), during which Christ's descent into hell and his reascent are taking place, is a preparation for a new resurrection event around 2133/2134, this time on the etheric level. This *etheric resurrection* will be of a profound significance for the following epoch of time, from 2133 onward, as the resurrection in A.D. 33 has been up until now. It is through uniting with the impulse of resurrection that, ultimately, evil will be overcome and the interior of Earth will become transformed.

In conclusion, therefore, the present period of time is one in which—through Christ, working in conjunction with human beings—the possibility is opened up of the transformation, in successive stages, of the interior of Earth. This transformation entails confrontation with the evil of the sub-earthly spheres, which is being released in successive stages.

Once a particular kind of evil gains entrance to civilization via a negative technological development or cultural impulse, it continues to work further until it is overcome—a prime example being drug addiction (as an example of a negative cultural impulse). Thus, humanity is called to awaken morally and spiritually to deal with the problems arising in this way. And the more clearly that this challenge is recognized as a struggle with evil, in which Christ has to be called upon in order to find deliverance from the evil, the better it will be. Underlying this call are the words of St. Paul, *"Not I, but Christ in me,"* indicating communion between the human self and the Self of Christ, the archetypal background to which is the descent into hell, as outlined here.

In this chapter it has not been possible to go into the other modes of communion with Christ, and our attention has been directed primarily to communion with the Christ Self in relation to the 12-year Jupiter rhythm. In my book *Christian Hermetic Astrology: The Star of the Magi and the Life of Christ*, I have outlined some aspects of communion with the astral body of Christ in connection with the 29 1/2-year Saturn rhythm, but the main content is concerned with communion with Christ's etheric body in relation to the 33 1/3-year rhythm. In the yearly *Christian Star Calendar* indications are given as to how to intensify this latter communion through living with the daily events in the world of stars, seen in correspondence with events in the life of Christ.

The Second Coming and the Approaching Trial of Humanity

In the foregoing reference was made to the Grail mystery comprising the sublime mystery of the four different kinds of communion with Christ. And just as the foregoing was concerned with communion of the human self with the Self of Christ, as expressed in St. Paul's words *"Not I, but Christ in me,"* so the following is concerned with communion of the purified astral body with Christ's astral body.

As described in the foregoing, we find the archetype of the communion of the human self with Christ's Self in Christ's descent into hell, down to the *Kingdom of the Mother*. For this was a descent of the Self of Christ alone, separated from the physical, etheric, and astral bodies. At the time of the Fall, the Mother withdrew into the darkness of the underworld, beneath the nine sub-earthly spheres of evil. In the ancient mystery centers, such as Eleusis in ancient Greece, a path of descent to the Mother (known to the Greeks as Demeter) was sought by way of ritual initiation. However, it was only through the Mystery of Golgotha, with Christ's descent to hell, that a path of descent to the Mother became opened up as a divine path. As described by Rudolf Steiner, *"The path is right, but it is very difficult. . . . If one passes through them [the nine sub-earthly spheres of evil] together with Christ, then the demons are unable to harm one, but otherwise they would be able to destroy one!"*[17] The path of descent to the Mother entails confrontation with the nine sub-earthly spheres of evil and is therefore a very difficult path. Nevertheless, it is precisely this path that is being opened up in the twentieth century through the Second Coming, with a new descent into hell by Christ having begun in 1945 (around the time of the explosion of the first atomic bomb). The cosmic rhythm underlying the descent into hell is the 12-year Jupiter rhythm.

Whereas the 12-year Jupiter rhythm is related to the Self of Christ, the rhythm of his etheric body is one of 33 1/3 years. As the life of Jesus Christ from birth to the Mystery of Golgotha lasted 33 1/3 years, all the events of his biography became inscribed into his etheric body. Since the Mystery of Golgotha the unfolding rhythm of 33 1/3 years of Christ's etheric body has played a major role in the spiritual history of humanity. Moreover, the content of the Four Gospels was inspired by this etheric body, which contains the Eternal Gospel. Since 1899, with the completion of the fifty-sixth 33 1/3-year cycle since the Mystery of Golgotha, Christ's etheric body has been working with renewed intensity in the twentieth century—in connection with the Second Coming, his manifestation in the etheric realm—and Rudolf Steiner's lectures *The Fifth Gospel* (1913) were inspired from this source. We are now nearing completion (in September 1999) of the fifty-ninth 33 1/3-year cycle since the Mystery of Golgotha, and then the sixtieth cycle will begin. The human being's transformed etheric body is able to enter into communion with the etheric body of Christ.

However, it is especially the communion of the purified astral body with Christ's astral body that is the central theme of the following. The purified astral body is known in the East as *manas*, and we find an historical archetype of the communion under consideration here in the "manna communion" of the people of Israel in the wilderness. In the Biblical account it is emphasized that manna was a product of the night (Exod. 16:6-13). At night the human self and astral body separate from the physical and etheric bodies during sleep. Normally the human being is not conscious of this sojourn in the astral body each night. However, through purification of the astral body the human being may become spiritually conscious during the night, and the wealth of experience thereby undergone bestows new strength upon him or her. This is the essence of manna communion which arises through the development of manas (the purified astral body). In the case of the people of Israel, into which Christ incarnated, the manna communion in the wilderness was an expression of the approaching Incarnation. Since the Mystery of Golgotha this mode of communion is possible if, through union of the human self with the Christ Self (*"Not I, but Christ in me"*), the

Christianized human self works purifyingly upon the astral body, transforming the latter into manas. An example of this we find historically in St. Francis of Assisi. The spiritual power exerted by St. Francis over wild animals bears witness to the transformation and purification of his own animal nature (astral body). The astral body thus purified becomes capable of entering into communion with Christ's astral body. What does this signify?

Just as Christ's etheric body is the bearer of the Eternal Gospel mirrored (in part) in the Four Gospels, so Christ's astral body is the bearer of the Eternal Apocalypse, part of which is mirrored in the Apocalypse of St. John (Book of Revelation). There Christ appeared to St. John with *"seven stars in his right hand"* (Rev. 1:16), symbolizing the seven planetary forces underlying the astral body. The entire symbolism of the Book of Revelation relates to the *"night consciousness"* that awakens through purification of the astral body, which then is able to enter into communion with Christ's astral body—as exemplified by St. John.

As the rhythm of Christ's etheric body is exactly 33 1/3 years, which was the length of the life of Christ Jesus on Earth, what is the rhythm of Christ's astral body? In order to answer this question, it is helpful to think of the following analogy. As described in my book *Hermetic Astrology, Vol. II: Astrological Biography*, the human being's destiny on Earth is prepared in the period between conception and birth. At the moment of birth, destiny begins to unfold in 7-year periods, whereby the first 7-year period is prepared during the first lunar sidereal month (27 1/3 days) of the embryonic period, the destiny of the second 7-year period is prepared during the second lunar sidereal month of the embryonic period, and so on. Hence there exists a clear correspondence between the embryonic period (conception to birth) and the course of life (birth to death), which gives rise to the human being's astrological biography.

Now, the moment of the baptism in the Jordan can be likened to the *conception* of Christ and the resurrection on Easter Sunday morning can be thought of as the moment of *birth* of the Risen One. By way of analogy, the period from the baptism to the resurrection, which lasted 1290 days, was the *embryonic period* of the Christ impulse, which has been at work since the Mystery of Golgotha. And just as human destiny unfolds in 7-year periods from the moment of birth onward, so the Christ impulse is unfolding historically according to a certain rhythm. What is this rhythm?

It is a much longer rhythm than the 7-year rhythm underlying the unfolding of human destiny. Let us recall that there is a correspondence between each 27 1/3-day lunar sidereal month of the embryonic period and each 7-year period of human life. Similarly, there is a correspondence between the "embryonic period" of 1290 days of the ministry of Christ and the rhythm underlying the unfolding of the Christ impulse historically. This correspondence is such that one day of Christ's ministry corresponds to 29 1/2 years historically. Those readers who are familiar with astronomy will recognize here the Saturn rhythm of 29 1/2 years, this being the period required by Saturn to make one orbit of the sidereal zodiac, just as the Sun's period is one year and Jupiter's period is twelve years. In fact, 29 1/2 years is the rhythm of Christ's astral body. How may this be understood?

Again it is by way of analogy that we may come to understand the relationship between the 29 1/2-year rhythm of Christ's astral body and the 33 1/3-year rhythm of his etheric body. For the human being there is an analogy here with the 27 1/3-day lunar sidereal month and the 29 1/2-day lunar synodic month. The Moon takes 27 1/3 days to complete one orbit of the sidereal zodiac. This rhythm relates to the astral (sidereal) world and, correspondingly, to the human astral body. On the other hand, the Moon's synodic period of 29 1/2 days is the length of time taken for the Moon to complete a cycle of its phases, e.g., New Moon to New Moon. This rhythm belongs to the etheric world and thus relates to the human etheric body. The difference between these two periods (a little more than two days) is the length of time taken *"in order that what we experience in our soul may be imprinted by the astral body upon the etheric."*[18] There is an analogy here with the 29 1/2-year rhythm of Christ's astral body and the 33 1/3-year rhythm of his etheric body. The difference between these two periods (just over 3 1/2 years) closely corresponds to the 3 1/2 years (1290 days) of Christ's ministry.

The point to bear in mind is that each day lived through by Christ during his ministry prepared the working of the Christ impulse for one "Saturn day" of 29 1/2 years in history, in the sense that Christ's judgment of each day became inscribed into his astral body, and from the time of the Mystery of Golgotha this working of the Christ impulse in history has been unfolding parallel to Saturn's orbit of the sidereal zodiac. As an example, let us consider the period of temptation known as the *"forty days in the wilderness."* It was on the evening of the Sabbath, 28 1/3 days after the baptism in the Jordan, that Christ Jesus began his forty days of fasting in the wilderness. The entire forty days was a period of temptation, which culminated with the final temptation—the meeting with Satan, who demanded that Christ turn stones into bread—towards the end of the thirty-ninth day.[19] (Here it must be borne in mind that the "day" in the Jewish calendar begins at dusk and lasts until sunset of the following day.) Christ's judgment of these forty days of temptation became inscribed into his astral body, the content of which has been unfolding historically according to the correspondence: one day to 29 1/2 years. Knowing this correspondence, we can arrive at an exact dating of the historical period of temptation of humanity.

Firstly, when did the historical period of temptation start? Since the forty days in the wilderness commenced 28 1/3 days after the baptism in the Jordan, these 28 1/3 days have to be multiplied by 29 1/2. We arrive at 836. This is the number of years after the Mystery of Golgotha that the historical period of temptation began. Since the Mystery of Golgotha took place in A.D. 33, this means that in A.D. 869 (33 + 836) the period of temptation of humanity began. Many readers will recognize the significance of this date. In 869 there took place the eighth Ecumenical Council (the fourth Council of Constantinople), which condemned Photius, who was made responsible for the schism between the Eastern and Western Church. It was at this historical point that Christianity began to lose sight of a truly spiritual conception of the human being. Seen against the background of Christ's ministry, 869 was the moment in the history of Christianity of *"entering into the wilderness"* and the *"start of the temptation of humanity."* Where do we stand now in relation to this period of humanity's temptation?

This period began with Saturn in sidereal Sagittarius in 869 and lasts forty revolutions of Saturn around the sidereal zodiac—ending with Saturn in Sagittarius in 2047. As described in the foregoing, this is close in time to 2040, when Christ on his path of descent through the sub-earthly spheres reaches the deepest level of descent, then to begin his ascent.

The year 2047 denotes the end of the period of humanity's temptation. And just as at the end of Christ's forty days in the wilderness *"Angels came and ministered to him"* (Matt. 4:11), so by the time of the middle of the next century there will be a ministering of Angels to humanity, for those who overcome temptation.

But when will the trial of humanity take place signified by the meeting with Satan at the culmination of the forty days in the wilderness? Cosmically this encounter between Christ and Satan was signified by the conjunction between the Sun and Pluto at 9° Sagittarius (in the sidereal zodiac) toward the end of the thirty-ninth day in the wilderness.[20] Now, as it happens, Pluto will reach 9° Sagittarius in the year 2010. Considering that the end of the thirty-ninth Saturn revolution since 869 will be in 2018 (during which year Saturn will cross 9° Sagittarius three times), the arrival of Pluto at 9° Sagittarius in 2010 will cosmically commemorate the encounter of Christ Jesus with Satan in the wilderness. How may this be interpreted?

According to Rudolf Steiner (1861-1925), just as Christ incarnated into Jesus two thousand years ago, so Ahriman (Satan) will also incarnate into a human form, and this will take place not long after the start of the third millennium, i.e., soon after the year 2000. This is known in Christian tradition as the incarnation of Antichrist. There are many prophecies concerning this, mostly derived from Christ's own words:

> *So when you see the abomination of desolation spoken of by the prophet Daniel, standing in the holy place . . . then there will be great tribulation, such as has not been from the beginning of the world until now, no, and never will be. And if those days had not been shortened, no human being would be saved; but for the sake of the elect those days will be shortened. Then if anyone says to you, "Lo, here is the Christ!" or "There he is!" do not believe it. For false Christs and false prophets will arise and show great signs and wonders, so as to lead astray, if possible, even the elect . . .* (Matt. 24:15,21-24).

The reference to the prophet Daniel is with respect to Daniel's prophecy concerning the city of Jerusalem (the *"holy place"*), where Daniel speaks of a *"prince who is to come [who] shall destroy the city and the sanctuary. . . ;*

desolations are decreed" (Dan. 9:26) Here Daniel is referring to the "prince of this world" (Satan).

In Vladimir Soloviev's inspired work *A Short Narrative About Antichrist*, published at Easter, 1900, he describes the false Christ (Antichrist) who, in league with the false prophet (the magician Apollyon), becomes emperor of the world and establishes his residence in Jerusalem. Among Apollyon's magical powers is the ability to make fire come down from heaven. This is a clear allusion to the two-horned beast referred to in the thirteenth chapter of the Book of Revelation. In fact, it is in the Book of Revelation that we find an account of the reign of Antichrist, the "beast," who is aided by the two-horned beast:

> *The two-horned beast exercises all the authority of the first beast in its presence, and makes the earth and its inhabitants worship the [first beast]. . . Men worshipped the first beast, saying, "Who is like the beast, and who can fight against it?" And the beast was given a mouth uttering haughty and blasphemous words, and it was allowed to exercise authority for forty-two months* (Rev. 13:12,4-5).

Regarding the Apocalypse as an account of the unfolding of the Christ impulse—insofar as it mirrors the content of Christ's astral body, unfolding historically in the Saturn-rhythm of 29 1/2 years—the Book of Revelation obviously must depict the encounter with Satan. For Christ Jesus this occurred toward the end of his thirty-ninth day in the wilderness. As the forty days in the wilderness started 28 1/3 days after the baptism in the Jordan, the encounter with Satan was about 67 days (28 + 39 = 67) into his ministry. Multiplying by 29 1/2 and adding to A.D. 33, we find that humanity's encounter with Satan—known traditionally as the coming of Antichrist—occurs in the period around 2010, when Pluto is again at 9° Sagittarius, where it was at the temptation of Christ in the wilderness (67 x 29 1/2 + 33 = 2010).

It is precisely the meeting with Antichrist that is depicted in the thirteenth chapter of the Book of Revelation. Satan, the dragon, gives his authority to the beast, i.e., he incarnates into a human form and becomes the beast, known in the tradition as Antichrist. The beast is allowed to exercise authority for forty-two months, which can be interpreted as signifying that Antichrist is allowed to gain world dominion (as emperor or *"prince of this world"*) and for a certain period of time (*"forty-two months"*) is allowed to tempt humanity into accepting him as the Messiah. According to the account of the Apocalypse, he is aided by the two-horned beast whose number is 666.

In his lectures published as *The Apocalypse of St. John*, Rudolf Steiner refers to 666 as the number of the Sun-Demon, Sorath. (Sorath is spelled in Hebrew: Samech, Vau, Resh, Tau—having the numerical value 60 + 6 + 200 + 400 = 666.) The Sun-Demon, Sorath, is the inspirer of black magic. And in Soloviev's account of the reign of Antichrist, he is helped by a magician (Apollyon) who is able to wield magical powers. In other words, just as one particular human being, by becoming a vehicle for Satan, will emerge as Antichrist, the beast, so will another human being act under the inspiration of Sorath as a wielder of black magic *"to make the earth and its inhabitants worship the first beast."* This second human being is *"the false prophet who in its [the beast's] presence had worked the signs by which he deceived those who had received the mark of the beast"* (Rev. 19:20).

Looking to the year 2010—as a rough orientation as to when the trial of humanity through the "world emperor" and his "magician" (the false prophet) will take place—it is clear that the two human beings spoken of here must already have been born before the year 2000. In fact a definite date for the birth of Antichrist was communicated by the American clairvoyant Jeane Dixon in her book *My Life and Prophecies*. In this book she refers to a vision she had of the birth of Antichrist at sunrise on February 5, 1962, at a place in the Middle East —a matter of hours after a total eclipse of the Sun in the sidereal sign of Capricorn. There was indeed a most spectacular alignment of planets in Capricorn at this time of the birth of Antichrist as indicated by Jeane Dixon, with Saturn, Jupiter, Mars, Venus, the Sun, Mercury, and the Moon aligned with the Moon's Node in Capricorn. The last time such a grand conjunction of the seven visible planets occurred was in 1524. If the future *"World President"* was actually born in 1962, then in 2010 he will be forty-eight years old, at the height of his power.

In conversation many years ago, Willi Sucher (1902-1985), pioneer of astrosophy, a new star wisdom, indicated that he had done research into Jeane Dixon's vision and found it quite plausible. Willi Sucher even identified the place of birth as Tobruk, Libya. When asked about the significance of the planetary alignment in Capricorn, he replied:

> In antiquity Capricorn was called the "gateway of the gods," and what better moment could Antichrist choose to be born than when all the planets are aligned in front of Capricorn, blocking the gateway to the spiritual world, in order to establish his rulership in a world of materialism, cutting off humanity from all spirituality.

Whether or not Jeane Dixon's vision is true remains to be seen. What is striking is the remarkable parallel between her vision and that of Soloviev. Although she does not mention a "magician," she does refer to powerful friends—among the political leaders of the United States—who will help Antichrist come to power. And she also speaks of Antichrist establishing his center of activity in Jerusalem. Against this background the political events in the Middle East, especially in connection with Israel, take on a new significance. It is no wonder that the Middle East is such a center of tension. And a figure such as the dictator of Iraq appears as a pawn in a much more complex game, preparing the way for the new world order that Antichrist is intending to usher in. The Gulf War may thus be seen as a stage in the chain of events leading toward this new world order. Here it may be mentioned that at the outbreak of the Gulf War there was a conjunction of the Sun with Saturn in the Moon's node, reminding us of the temptation in the desert (as remarked upon in the *Christian Star Calendar*, January, 1991). The Gulf War lasted almost exactly forty days, as with the forty days of temptation, and it took place in the wilderness (being named *Desert Storm*). Without going into details, we can see the deeper significance of the Gulf War against the background of preparing the way for Antichrist.

For humanity as a whole the question is raised: Christ or Antichrist? This is the essence of the approaching trial that will be presented to humankind by the emergence of Antichrist upon the world stage. This trial has to come for the whole of humanity, just as Christ had to encounter Satan toward the end of the forty days in the wilderness. At that time it was necessary, for it was only through the overcoming of temptation that Christ cleared the way for the unfolding of his mission.

The same holds true now with respect to the future mission of the Christ impulse for the Earth and humankind. Nevertheless, the severity and enormity of the approaching trial of humanity must not be underestimated. In Christ's own words:

> *Take heed that no one leads you astray. For many will come in my name, saying, "I am the Christ," and they will lead many astray. And you will hear of wars and rumors of wars. . . . For nation will rise against nation, and kingdom against kingdom, and there will be famines and earthquakes in various places. . . . Then there will be great tribulation, such as has not been from the beginning of the world until now, no, and never will be* (Matt. 24:4-7, 21).

In connection with these words we may think of the Gulf War; of famine in Ethiopia, Sudan, Mozambique, and elsewhere; of the devastation wrought by cyclones in Bangladesh and Japan and by flooding in China; and of the earthquakes in Costa Rica, Georgia, the Philippines, Japan, and California. Yet we may also take consolation from Christ's words, for he spoke them to the disciples in response to their question: *"What will be the signs of your coming?"* In other words, we are now living in the age of the Second Coming, and all the trials and tribulations of our time may be seen against the background of this event. Indeed, it is this event that can give us the spiritual strength to meet and overcome all, including the great trial that will be presented by Antichrist. And it is for this reason that it is of such importance to occupy ourselves with Christ's Second Coming, to find a relationship to this event and to find a connection with Christ himself along the path of communion with him. There are various approaches that may be followed, and here it is above all the path of communion (through purification of the astral body) with Christ's astral body that has been at the center of our considerations. For this path holds the key to the mysteries of the Apocalypse and to reading the apocalyptic nature of the signs of the times in which we live. Along this path the incarnation of Antichrist appears as the shadow side of the Second Coming—the one event taking place on the physical plane of existence and the other in the etheric realm accessible only to spiritual vision. For humanity as a whole it is a matter of choice, the choice being: Christ or Antichrist? This is a choice between good and evil, between a spiritual outlook and materialism. In the last analysis it is a question of whether humanity will recognize and choose Christ as the Risen One, who through the resurrection celebrated the triumph of the spiritual. In the words of Soloviev:

> We have only one firm support: the true resurrection. We know that the struggle between good and evil is being fought out not only in the soul and in society but also deeper—in the physical world. And from the past we know already of a victory of the Good—the personal resurrection of One. . . . The kingdom of God is the kingdom of victorious life, triumphant through the resurrection, and here—in this triumphant life—lies also the true and ultimate good that has to be brought to realization. Here lies the entire power and the whole work of Christ. [21]

Tribulation and the Second Coming

To summarize the foregoing reflections upon Christ's Second Coming, we have looked at three rhythms: the $33\,^1/_3$-year rhythm of Christ's etheric body; the $29\,^1/_2$-year rhythm of Christ's astral body; and the 12-year rhythm of Christ's Self. Through an understanding of these three rhythms, we are able to gain insight into the apocalyptic nature of the time in which we are living.

For example, in connection with the rhythm of Christ's etheric body, we are approaching a significant period of time as we draw near to the end of the twentieth century. The $33\,^1/_3$-year rhythm derives from the life of Jesus Christ, extending from birth in Bethlehem to the resurrection. The most important time during these $33\,^1/_3$ years was the period of $3\,^1/_2$ years from the baptism in the Jordan to the resurrection. Likewise, with the rhythmical recurrence of the $33\,^1/_3$-year rhythm—which, since the start of the New Age in 1899, has become the central rhythm of the wave of Christ's Second Coming—it is the last $3\,^1/_2$ years that are of major importance. These last $3\,^1/_2$ years signify a reliving, on the etheric plane, of the ministry of Jesus Christ from the baptism to the Mystery of Golgotha. The last $3\,^1/_2$-year period was from October 27, 1962 (baptism) to May 9, 1966 (resurrection), and the new $3\,^1/_2$-year period (always comprising 1290 days, this being the interval from the baptism to the resurrection) extends from February 24, 1996 (baptism) to September 6, 1999 (resurrection). We are thus living in a very important time—the last $3\,^1/_2$ years of the twentieth century—during which a remarkable opportunity for a more intensive attunement to Christ's presence in the etheric world is opening up. This $3\,^1/_2$-year period began in 1996 and was announced by Comet Hyakutake. The second year (1997) of the $3\,^1/_2$-year period was proclaimed by Comet Hale-Bopp. The coming of the comets to announce the Second Coming was indicated in Christ's words about the signs accompanying his return: *"And there will be signs in sun and moon and stars"*(Luke 21:25). At the same time, there is also a renewed attack upon humanity—in the form of temptation—as a counterimpulse to the impulse of Christ's Second Coming, just as the temptation to take drugs broke out in epidemic form during the last 3 1/2-year period (1962-1966).

From the standpoint of the unfolding 29 1/2-year period (Saturn rhythm) of Christ's astral body, the time of the emergence of Antichrist, expected shortly after the start of the third millennium, is approaching. This event signifies the culmination of humanity's "temptation in the wilderness," which began in A.D. 869, around the time of the eighth Ecumenical Council. Just as the way for Jesus was prepared by John the Baptist, so the way for Antichrist will be prepared by the false prophet, who will be endowed with magical powers and who will act in the name of the two-horned beast, whose number is 666. The year 1998 (= 3 x 666) indicates the time when the influence of the false prophet will be especially noticeable, in preparation for the emergence of Antichrist—acting in the name of Satan, the dragon—not long after the year 2000. The last day (fortieth day) of humanity's temptation in the wilderness, by which time the temptation presented to humanity by Antichrist hopefully will have been overcome, extends from 2018 to 2047, corresponding to one orbit of Saturn around the sidereal zodiac (from Sagittarius to Sagittarius). Then a new relationship between humanity and the angelic kingdom will open up, just as on the fortieth day in the wilderness, having overcome temptation, *"Angels came and ministered to him"* (Matt. 4:11).

With respect to the 12-year rhythm of the Self of Christ, it is the descent into hell that holds the key. A new descent into hell has been underway since 1945, with the descent through each sub-earthly sphere lasting 12 years (Jupiter rhythm). In a certain sense, this began already in 1933, the 12-year period from 1933 to 1945 being related to the first sub-earthly sphere, connected with the Mineral Earth (thought of as an eggshell), which became cracked open by the explosion of the atomic bomb in 1945. The descent through the remaining eight sub-earthly spheres will last until 2040, and then the reascent of Christ's Self will begin, returning to the Mineral Earth ("eggshell") in 2134. Here, we may look to a new resurrection event, connected with the reunion of Christ's Self with the other bodies of the Christ. The descent into hell signifies the *"opening of the gates of hell"* for humanity.

Thus, it is clear that the New Age, the Age of the Second Coming, is at the same time the Age of the Apocalypse, entailing a confrontation with evil. And who can doubt, viewed against the background of two world wars and all the other catastrophic events in the twentieth century, that with the twentieth century, humanity has entered into the Apocalyptic Age? In apocalyptic language, we are now living in the time of *tribulation.*

> *Immediately after the tribulation of those days the sun will be darkened and the moon will not give its light, and the stars will fall from heaven, and the powers of the heavens will be shaken; then shall appear the sign of the Son of man in heaven. . . .* (Matt. 24:29-30).

In these words of Jesus Christ—spoken to his disciples in response to their question, *"What will be the sign of your coming and of the close of the age?"*—he refers to the *"tribulation of those days."* What is meant here by *tribulation*? Tribulation means "severe affliction." In Matthew 24, this word is used three times by Christ in his answer to this question of the disciples:

> In verse 9: *"Then they will deliver you up to tribulation, and put you to death; and you will be hated by all nations for my name's sake."* Here Christ prophesies that severe affliction will be brought upon the disciples at the hands of their persecutors. Such is happening in various parts of the world today, where many are being persecuted.

> In verse 21: *"Then there will be great tribulation, such as has not been from the beginning of the world until now, no, and never will be."* Here the word is used in a more general sense as "a time of suffering." The start of this time is indicated by Christ's prophetic words: *"Nation will rise against nation, and kingdom against kingdom, and there will be famines and earthquakes in various places: all this is but the beginning of the sufferings"* (verses 7-8). The scourge of militant nationalism is strong on the Earth today.

> In verse 29 (quoted above): The preceding *"tribulation of those days"* is indicated by cosmic events culminating with the appearance of *"the sign of the Son of man in heaven."*

But what is the sign of the Son of man in heaven? On the basis of a true understanding of the zodiac—without going into detail—there is good reason to propose that *"the sign of the Son of man in heaven"* is indicated by the entrance of the vernal point into the constellation (sidereal sign) of Aquarius, which will take place in A.D. 2375.[22] This astronomical event is evidently connected with Christ's Second Coming and also denotes the *"close of the age"*—namely the end of the astronomical age of Pisces = A.D. 215-2375. If this be accepted here—at least as a working hypothesis—it means that the period of *tribulation* will last until the start of the Age of Aquarius in A.D. 2375. But when does it begin?

In the Gospel of Matthew, the signs of the *"beginnings of the sufferings"* are referred to by Jesus Christ as *war, famine, and earthquake.* A clear and realistic view of the twentieth century reveals it to be—and to have been (not merely via the heightened focus of media attention)—unprecedented as a time of war, famine, and earthquake, with every indication that these are on the increase. The Gulf War, the war in Yugoslavia, and the Kosovo conflict, the wars in various African countries, the famines in Somalia, Ethiopia, North Korea, and Southern Sudan, the earthquakes in Indonesia (Flores Island), Japan (Kobe), Italy (Assisi), and Columbia (Armenia) are immediate examples. Many more can be given. We need only think of the two World Wars, the awful African and Asian famines, the very powerful San Francisco earthquake (8.3 on the Richter scale) of April 18, 1906, which killed over 1000 people and caused untold damage, and the devastating earthquake (6.4 on the Richter scale) on September 30, 1993, east of Bombay, which killed an estimated 20,000 people. There are certainly grounds for judging the twentieth century to be the time of the *"beginning of the sufferings"* prophesied by Christ some two millennia ago.

But the twentieth century is not only a time of catastrophe. It is also a time of spiritual awakening, when a new spiritual light is beginning to shine in. What stands behind this?

Modern spiritual science confirms the view of Hindu chronology that A.D. 1899 marked the end of Kali Yuga, the Dark Age, and the start of the

Age of Light. As described in the Foreword, the arising of the Age of Light has to do with the Second Coming of Christ. Further, in St. Matthew we read, *"Then shall appear the sign of the Son of man in heaven, and then shall all the tribes of the earth mourn, and they shall see the Son of man coming in the clouds of heaven with power and great glory"* (24:30). The *"sign of the Son of man in heaven"* and the Second Coming—*"the Son of man coming in the clouds of heaven"*—are here connected with one another. What is the nature of this connection?

Here only a rough outline can be given. Let us start with the teaching of Hindu chronology: Kali Yuga, the Dark Age, began in 3102 B.C. (= -3101) and lasted 5000 years until 1899. Then the Satya Yuga began, the Age of Light, which will last half as long as Kali Yuga, i.e., 2500 years, until 4399. It is the Age of Light that is the true New Age. As elaborated elsewhere, this New Age could be designated as the "Age of the Second Coming" of the Cosmic Christ.[23]

However, this New Age is not identical with the Age of Aquarius. For, with the entrance of the vernal point into Aquarius, the Aquarian Age will start in A.D. 2375, and will last 2160 years until A.D. 4535 (2160 years being the length of time taken for the vernal point to regress through the 30° of the sidereal sign of Aquarius at the rate of precession of 1° in 72 years).

Nevertheless, most of the Aquarian Age falls within the Age of Light, the New Age; and the ends of these two Ages nearly coincide. The difference of 136 years between 4399 and 4535 amounts to less than 2° of precession (2 x 72 = 144).

Thus, the 2500-year New Age of Light includes a period of 476 years belonging to the tail end of the Piscean Age—namely from 1899-2375—plus a period of 2024 years, from 2375-4399, approximately coinciding with the Aquarian Age. In terms of this perspective, when interpreted in the light of the above-quoted words of Jesus Christ concerning his Second Coming, the first 476 years of the New Age comprise the time of tribulation, leading up to the appearance of the *"sign of the Son of man in heaven,"* which we have identified with the start of the Age of Aquarius, the Waterman. We can summarize this in the following approximate formulation:

NEW AGE (1899-4399) = TRIBULATION (1899-2375) + AQUARIAN AGE (2375-4399*) (*actually 4535), where:

NEW AGE = Age of Second Coming (manifestation of Jesus Christ as the Risen One in the Earth's biosphere—*"in the clouds"*);

TRIBULATION = period of upheaval and transition, entailing suffering (wars, famines, earthquakes); onset of Christ's Second Coming perceptible to those with spiritually awakened vision (to which many have testified in the twentieth century);

AQUARIAN AGE = appearance of *"the sign of the Son of man in heaven"* (entrance of the vernal point into Aquarius); Christ's Second Coming becomes generally perceptible (*"all the tribes of the earth will mourn, and they will see the Son of man coming in the clouds of heaven").*

Consequently, there is a definite connection between the New Age and the Age of Aquarius: for the Aquarian Age and the latter part of the New Age virtually coincide. But knowledge of this connection would be incomplete if we did not take account of the first part of the New Age: the period of tribulation, in which we are now living.

Tribulation is characterized on the one hand by wars, famines, and earthquakes, and on the other hand by the spiritual awakening to the presence of the Risen One in the kingdoms of Nature, within the Earth's biosphere. This is indicated by Jesus Christ himself: *"For as the lightning comes out of the east and shines even unto the west, so also shall the coming of the Son of man be"* (Matt. 24:27). As Rudolf Steiner elaborates:

> Only an understanding of the Mystery of Golgotha can enable us to morally sense the whole of Nature. If one then looks up to the clouds and sees lightning shooting forth, then one will be able to see Christ therein in His etheric form—"with the clouds"—i.e., He is coming in this spiritual form with the elements. This vision will emerge at some time for every human being, be it sooner or later.[24]

The development of a moral sense for Nature is helpful for the vision of the coming Son of man. It also helps us gain a new relationship to the increasing number of natural catastrophes. The period 1991-1995, centered around the year 1993, is particularly striking in this respect. For during this time, the planets Uranus and Neptune drew close together, entering into conjunction slowly from 1991 to 1993, and separating again slowly from 1993 to 1995. During the whole of 1993 Uranus and Neptune were in close conjunction with one another (conjoining three times in sidereal Sagittarius, on February 2, August 19, and October 25).[25]

Uranus and Neptune—as also Pluto—are connected with specific subterranean forces.[26] These forces are particularly active in various natural catastrophes such as earthquakes and volcanic eruptions. A striking finding is that, at the San Francisco earthquake of 1906, Uranus and Neptune stood in opposition to one another: Uranus at 15° Sagittarius and Neptune in mid-Gemini at 14 1/2°. (All longitudes are given in degrees in the signs/constellations of the sidereal zodiac.)

Uranus was at 18° Sagittarius, drawing close to Neptune at 21 1/2° Sagittarius, on the morning of June 12, 1991, when Mt. Pinatubo (Philippines) erupted, sending a vast cloud of volcanic ash and dust into the atmosphere, visible over sixty miles away, and venting nineteen million tons of sulfur dioxide in a plume that gradually engirdled the Earth, causing a one degree drop in the global temperature between June 1991 and May 1992. Uranus at 22° and Neptune at 23° Sagittarius were still closer—with the Moon in opposition in Gemini—when the earthquake struck off Flores Island, Indonesia, on December 12, 1992, as mentioned above. When the recent massive earthquake (7.5 on the Richter scale) shook Hokkaido, North Japan, on the evening of January 15, 1993, Mercury at 25 1/2° Sagittarius was conjunct Uranus and Neptune, both at 24° Sagittarius.

A moral experience of Mother Nature reveals an earthquake as a manifestation of fear or an outburst of anger. Having been badly mistreated and ruthlessly exploited at the hands of human beings—especially since the scientific-industrial-technological revolution that began in earnest around the time of the last conjunction between Uranus and Neptune (a triple conjunction in 1821 in sidereal Sagittarius)—Nature is beginning to react more strongly. Not just earthquakes and volcanic eruptions, but also hurricanes, tornadoes, typhoons, flash floods, cold snaps, and other extremes and disruptions of the climate are Nature's response to the ravages she has suffered through humanity's misdeeds since the advent of the industrial-technological age. What, then, can be done, in the face of the increasing tide of natural catastrophes in the period of *tribulation*?

We are called upon to develop a new, morally permeated relationship to Nature. Everything depends on this, which can lead to the true vision of the coming of the Son of man. Even in the midst of the most violent storm, he may reveal himself in the flashes of lightning and in the pulses of the warmth ether (thermosphere) of the Earth. We ought not to forget that Jesus Christ, when *"there arose a great storm on the sea . . . rebuked the wind and the sea, and there was a great calm"* (Matt. 8:24-26); nor that *"the earth shook and the rocks were split"* (Matt. 27:51) in an earthquake at the moment of his death on the cross, which tore open the earth at the foot of the cross as he descended into hell, into the interior of the Earth. Truly, the Risen Christ is Lord of the Elements. And just as he came walking on the water to the disciples and stilled the waves, so he may come walking through the elements of Nature—fire, air, water, earth—at any time, even in the hour of catastrophe, as an Angel guiding to safety. Trust and a mood of serenity in the face of tribulation are called for here. For all fear and anxiety concerning that which comes from the future serve only to wrap the human being in dark clouds of emotions, hindering the very connection with the spiritual world that is needed in order to be guided to safety.

Even though Sodom and Gomorrah were destroyed when the Lord rained down *"fire and brimstone"* on account of the *"wicked sinners"* living in these cities, Angels came to Lot the evening before and guided him and his family to safety (Gen. 19). If Lot had experienced terror at the impending destruction, his fear could have hindered the angelic guidance he needed in order to be led out of the doomed city of Sodom. And so it will be during the present period of tribulation for those living in the modern day equivalents of Sodom and Gomorrah, and for all of us living in areas threatened by natural catastrophe. The appropriate mood or quality of soul that is called for in this time of tribulation is wonderfully expressed in the following meditation:

> Is there anything that can pour some certainty about the future into our souls? It is what we may call the feeling of devoted acceptance of what enters our souls from the hidden future, and it can

only work properly if it arises as an attitude of prayer. . . . If we look to the future with fear and anxiety, we strangle our development and hamper the free unfolding of our soul forces. Nothing so obstructs this development as anxiety about what may come to the soul from the future. . . . No matter what might come, no matter what the next hour or day might bring, were it unknown to us, we could not alter it by fear or anxiety. We should wait for it, therefore, in complete inner peace and utter tranquility. . . . To give ourselves up to the divine wisdom of events, to be certain in our thoughts, feelings, and impulses that what will be must be and that it will have its good effects somewhere, to call forth this feeling in the soul and to live it in our words and ideas is . . . the prayer of devoted acceptance.[27]

Living in Apocalyptic Times

(A lecture given at The Boulder Anthroposophical Institute Conference: The Tasks of Anthroposophy in America at the End of the Millennium, Boulder, Colorado, August 2, 1996. The Conference presenters were: René Querido, teacher and author; William Bento, pioneer in psychosophy; Robert Schiappacasse, astrosophical researcher; and Robert Powell.)

Let us look at these troubled times in which we are living, as we approach the end of the twentieth century. Of course the term "end of the twentieth century" is relative. As René Querido pointed out, one could say that from 1950 onward we are already going toward the end of the twentieth century. But certainly we are approaching a culmination, and it is indeed a very special moment in time during these last years leading up to the year 2000. It is a time of unprecedented significance.

In order to connect onto what René said yesterday evening and what William Bento referred to this morning, I would like to briefly recapitulate. René spoke of the three main problems or trials besetting humanity at the present time. These can be described as the mechanization of the spirit, the vegetabilizing of the soul, and the animalizing of the body. Let us now look at these from a somewhat different point of view, deepening and drawing attention to this subject from another perspective.

William spoke about geographical mysteries connected with the two American continents. He referred to the Saturn mysteries connected with the Americas—including North, Central, and South America. William was touching upon the mysteries of space, that the world can be looked at spiritually from different spatial perspectives. If we look at it from a spatial point of view, we see that there are profound differences between different regions of the world.

The perspective I would like to take now is more of a temporal point of view. In order to do this we need to take a broad view of things. To start with I would like to invite you to try and imagine a most beautiful flower; just inwardly picture a most beautiful flower. This will comprise the root going down beneath the earth, the stem, the leaves and the blossom. Such an image we can think of in connection with the lifework of Rudolf Steiner, the founder of Anthroposophy. We can think of the period up until the beginning of the twentieth century as the period of time when he was laying the foundation through his philosophical works and through his studies of Goethe, especially Goethe's world conception. It was here that he was elaborating a foundation for his later work. In terms of the flower image we can think of this as the root. Then something happened to him. He describes in his autobiography that in 1899 he had a Christ experience. This experience transformed him from being a philosopher concerned with the theory of knowledge into becoming a spiritual teacher. From this point onward we have the beginning of the emergence of Anthroposophy, and we can think of this as breaking through the ground soil, the beginning of the birth of the flower we might call Anthroposophy.

This signified the beginning of his extraordinary lecturing activity. As René pointed out, we find that Rudolf Steiner would often bring something completely new, sometimes touching upon it again at some later point in time and then never referring to it after that. So, in the course of his extensive lecturing activity—some 6,000 lectures—we find pearls of wisdom scattered through all these lectures without Rudolf Steiner's repeating himself. He was always bringing new knowledge, continual unfolding revelations of divine wisdom.

Here we can see the growth of the flower of Anthroposophy. This activity then began to bear fruit. We could think of the leaves emerging from it as the artistic activities he began in 1907 and then the practical activities he developed from 1917 onward. The flower began more and more to take shape and contour. Toward the end of the year 1923 there occurred the event known as the Christmas Foundation meeting, the spiritual founding of the Anthroposophical Society. With this event there took place the opening of the flower of Anthroposophy; everything had been leading toward this event. How may we conceive of this?

Rudolf Steiner indicated on several occasions that the whole of Anthroposophy is a preparation for the coming of Christ in what is known as the Second Coming. This he described as the coming of Christ in the etheric, in the world of the life forces. The world of Nature, which is permeated with etheric forces, is especially affected by this. Thus the whole of Anthroposophy is leading toward this event of the coming of Christ in the etheric. But who is Christ?

Christ is Divine Love. Everything that Rudolf Steiner brought as Anthroposophy—Anthroposophia—was preparing for this event of the breaking through of Divine Love, which took place at the Christmas Foundation Meeting with the laying of the Foundation Stone, the Stone of Love, into the hearts of those human beings who connect themselves with Anthroposophy. The word *Anthroposophia* signifies wisdom, wisdom of the human being (anthropos). *Sophia* is the Greek word for wisdom, the wisdom of Sophia, the Bride or Sister or Companion of the Christ. Sophia is the Being who is referred to in the Book of Revelation as the Bride of the Lamb. She accompanies Christ. There is an intimate interweaving between Sophia, Divine Wisdom, and Christ, Divine Love. And as Sergei Prokofieff has shown in his book on the Heavenly Sophia, Anthroposophia is an offspring of the Divine Sophia. We find aspects of the Divine Sophia in all the great religions and spiritual traditions. Where true wisdom lives, we find aspects of the Divine Sophia.

In Christianity, with the coming of the Christ 2000 years ago, we find the beginning of Divine Love. At that time John the Baptist prepared the way for Christ, proclaiming him as the Lamb of God. We see a similar preparation for the Second Coming of Christ beginning in the twentieth century, revealed in the activity of the Divine Sophia through Rudolf Steiner, who brought Anthroposophia to prepare the way for this coming of Christ. The Bride prepares the way for the coming of the Lamb (Christ). We have an incomplete picture of Anthroposophia if we don't see the other half of what Anthroposophia is really about. The other half is the Etheric Christ. When we think of the Etheric Christ we think of the other half of Anthroposophia. And a shining in of the Etheric Christ took place at the Foundation Stone meeting of 1923 with the laying of the Stone of Divine Love in human hearts.

This Stone of Love is clothed in the words of the Foundation Stone Meditation, which we are working with in eurythmy each morning. Through this meditation we are able to enter into a relationship with the Being of Anthroposophy. Rudolf Steiner spoke of the fact that he spiritually heard the words of the Foundation Stone Meditation from the Logos (Christ). The first verse of this meditation begins with the words, *"Human Soul, thou livest in the limbs."* The second verse begins, *"Human Soul, thou livest in the beat of heart and lung."* And the third verse opens with, *"Human Soul, thou livest in the resting head."* Here the Etheric Christ addresses the human soul in our will, in our feeling, and in our thinking.

This relates to the content of the first three verses of the Foundation Stone Meditation. The fourth verse is a response (formulated by Rudolf Steiner) to the Logos, the Etheric Christ, speaking to the human soul. This fourth verse is a meditation that is at the same time a prayer arising from the human being in response to the words of the Etheric Christ addressed to the soul. With the Christmas Foundation Meeting we begin to grasp something of the magnitude of what Anthroposophy is. We can begin to see that this flower really is only one side of what the Being of Anthroposophy is. The other side is the Spiritual Sun, the Christ, who shines in and illumines and fructifies this flower.

When we look at Anthroposophy we have to think to its other side, the light of the Spiritual Sun, the Etheric Christ, who is the other half of Anthroposophy. If we wish to understand Anthroposophy, and the tasks of Anthroposophy at the end of the twentieth century, we can start to do so if we begin to comprehend the work of the Etheric Christ in his coming in the etheric. As it says in the Book of Revelation, in the words of St. John, this is his coming in the clouds—the clouds being a suitable outer representation for the realm of life, the etheric. For the clouds bring rain, thus bringing life to Earth. Through this image we can begin to understand the coming of the Etheric Christ.

At this point, we need to enter into the mysteries of time, the unfolding of time. Robert Schiappacasse was kind enough to refer to my new book, *The Chronicle of the Living Christ*, in which I have summarized about ten years of research into the life of Christ and the rhythms of the life of

Christ. For an understanding of the coming of the Etheric Christ, the most important rhythm is the 33 1/3-year rhythm. This is the length of time from the birth of Jesus to the Mystery of Golgotha, a period of 33 1/3 years. All the events in the life of Christ—his biography—were inscribed into his etheric body during this period of 33 1/3 years. What took place at the death and resurrection of the Christ?

As with every human being at the time of death, the etheric body and higher members separate from the physical body. At this moment the human being is indwelling the etheric body and sees the content of the etheric body, which is the entire biography—all the images and pictures that are imprinted into the etheric body. The moment we separate from the physical body, we see our entire biography as a great panorama. Gradually these images of our life start to fade away as the etheric body begins to dissolve back into the etheric cosmos.

In the case of Christ Jesus, his etheric body had become completely transformed and spirit-permeated. It did not dissolve back into the cosmos after his death but remained intact, as a time organism—a time body—containing this rhythm of 33 1/3 years. The etheric body of Christ has continued to work through the course of history since that moment in time in the year A.D. 33. Just as, say for example, the planet Jupiter has a 12-year rhythm, Saturn a 29 1/2-year rhythm, the Sun a one-year rhythm—so here we have something akin to a planetary rhythm. However, this is not an external planet. It is a time rhythm that is part of the Christ Being and has been active since the year 33. We can follow this rhythm down through history. However, in order to grasp this rhythm we need to come to a comprehension of what took place after the resurrection of Christ Jesus.

Let us imagine the Garden of the Holy Sepulchre that Easter Sunday morning. Mary Magdalene came to the garden and was astonished to see that the stone had been rolled away from the tomb. The tomb was empty. She turned around and saw someone whom she thought was the gardener. When she spoke to him and he replied, she realized, "This is the Master." She went to touch him, and he said, *"Do not touch me, for I have not yet ascended to my Father, but go and tell the disciples that I will ascend to the Father."* With this, Christ Jesus was proclaiming his approaching ascent to the Kingdom of the Father, the ascent which began forty days later at Ascension. During these forty days Christ Jesus appeared over and over again to the circle of disciples. Some of these appearances are described in the Gospels, for example, the appearance that following evening to the ten apostles without Thomas; his appearance to Luke and Cleophas on the way to Emmaus; and his appearance to the eleven disciples, with Thomas, when Thomas was invited to touch his wounds. The Christ had the ability to manifest and disappear. He could come in through closed doors and leave the room again. He could even partake of food with the apostles. He ate fish with them on the northeast shore of the Sea of Galilee, as described in the last chapter of the Gospel of St. John. Then came Ascension Day when he appeared to the disciples together with the Virgin Mary and guided them around the city of Jerusalem, pointing out places that were of significance for his path of suffering. He went on ahead of them and ascended the Mount of Olives, becoming more and more radiant. He reached the top of the mountain at midday and became so radiantly bright—he was brighter than the midday Sun and above him there appeared a rainbow. He turned around, blessed the whole world and then disappeared, radiantly light, into a cloud of light from which there issued resounding tones like trumpets. Two Angels appeared out of the light and said to the disciples, *"O men of Galilee, why do you stand looking up to heaven for Jesus of Nazareth? He will appear again in the same way you have seen him going."* With this, the Angels were proclaiming the event of his Second Coming, the event of his reappearance. Knowledge of the $33\,^{1}/_{3}$-year rhythm enables us to find exactly when this reappearance is to take place.

Starting in the year 33, Christ Jesus began an ascent to the Kingdom of the Father. What is meant here is an ascent through the planetary spheres, which is the same as the journey of the soul in the life after death—through the Moon sphere, the realm of Angels; through the Mercury sphere, the realm of Archangels; and so on, through all the ranks of the spiritual hierarchies—through the ranks of the nine hierarchies, spending approximately one hundred years in the realm of each hierarchy. (One hundred years is three times $33\,^{1}/_{3}$.) Up to the year 133 was the first period between the years 33 and 133, during which took place the ascent of the Christ through the Moon sphere, the realm of Angels. Between 133 and 233 he passed through the realm of the Archangels, the

Mercury sphere. After the lapse of a further one hundred years (233-333) passing through the Venus sphere, the realm of the Spirits of Time, he entered the Sun sphere in the year 333. Rudolf Steiner often refers to the significance of the year 333. Looking at these dates in connection with the ascent of Christ through the planetary spheres, we can find corresponding events on earth below. Let us consider an example of this in connection with this last date.

Around 333 was the time when Christianity ceased to be persecuted in the Roman Empire. Emperor Constantine the Great allowed Christianity to flourish. He called the First Ecumenical Council of Christianity in the year 325. This event on Earth below corresponds more or less to the entrance of Christ into the Sun sphere above.

The passage of the Christ Being through the three hierarchical ranks of the Sun sphere—those of the Exusiai, Dynamis, and Kyriotetes—lasted until the year 633, when the Christ entered into the Mars sphere. The year 632 was that of the death of Mohammed. After this began the tremendous expansion of Islam, signifying a period of war throughout Christendom. This was mirrored on Earth below, corresponding to the passage of Christ through the Mars sphere. Then followed his passage through the Jupiter sphere. The year 732, coinciding more or less with the entrance of Christ into the Jupiter sphere, was when Charles Martel won the battle at Poitiers and drove back the Saracens from France. This led to the founding of the Carolingian dynasty and subsequent flourishing of the Carolingian renaissance, which signified the beginning of a new era for Christianity. It was during this period that Charlemagne became crowned, in the year 800. (Charlemagne was Charles Martel's grandson.)

The end of this Jupiter period, in the year 833, was the time when the Carolingian kingdom became divided between the four sons of Louis the Pious, the son of Charlemagne. Then followed the passage of Christ through the Saturn sphere, lasting until the year 933, coinciding with the entrance of Christ into the realm of the zodiac, the realm of the fixed stars, which is the outer manifestation of the Kingdom of God, beyond the nine hierarchies. In other words, after the passage through the Saturn sphere—the sphere of the Seraphim, the highest hierarchy—the Christ Being ascended into the Kingdom of the Father, coming to expression outwardly in the realm of the fixed stars. Here this rhythm unfolded through one more period of $33\ ^1/_3$ years (933-966), and during this time the life of Christ was inscribed as an archetype into the realm of the fixed stars. The year 966 signified the "midnight hour" in the Kingdom of the Father after the passage of the Christ through the ranks of the hierarchies. This was the turning point. Then began the descent of Christ, exactly mirroring his ascent. Initially this entailed a mirroring of the period (933-966), i.e., this meant one more period of $33\ ^1/_3$ years in the zodiacal realm (966-999). The year 999 marked the beginning of the descent of Christ through the planetary spheres of the hierarchies, first returning through the Saturn sphere (999-1099), the realm of the Seraphim. (See the figure on page iv of the Foreword.) In following this descent, again we find landmarks in the unfolding of the history of Christianity along this path of descent.

For example, in the year 1099 the leader of the first crusade, Godfrey of Bouillon, reconquered Jerusalem from the Saracens and was crowned King of Jerusalem in that year that coincided with the descent of the Christ from the Saturn sphere into the Jupiter sphere in A.D. 1099. We can follow the further passage of Christ down through the ranks of the hierarchies in the planetary spheres. Against this background each century acquires a particular coloring through this descent of Christ returning toward the Earth, reentering the aura of the Earth in the year 1899.

The descent of Christ through the realm of the Moon sphere took place between 1799 and 1899. The year 1799 saw a beginning of the Romantic movement through Novalis, who was a pioneer in Germany of that movement (Novalis died in 1801), and this century is called the Romantic Century. Perhaps the basic longing and striving of the Romantics was for Christ, who was not yet there, or was it for Sophia, accompanying Christ, whom they were really seeking? For, as Owen Barfield believes, as he describes so clearly in his book *Romanticism Comes of Age*, what the Romantics were really looking for was Anthroposophy.

The year 1899 was the year in which Rudolf Steiner had his Christ experience. He became transformed from being a philosopher, preoccupied with the theory of knowledge, into an apostle of the Etheric Christ. Rudolf Steiner also described that with the year 1899 there began the New Age. As far as I know, he was the first person to use the term *New Age*, which is now used everywhere.

He dates the beginning of the New Age to 1899, and he brings this New Age into connection with the appearance of Christ in the etheric. He describes the essence of this appearance as one in which the Etheric Christ is leading us to Shamballa—to a new experience of the lost kingdom of paradise, the golden realm of paradise, which has sunk to the center of the Earth, the heart of Earth. This golden globe in the middle of Earth is called, in the Orient, Shamballa. It is called in Christian esotericism the Kingdom of the Divine Mother, the heart of Mother Earth. Thus the descent of Christ now, and his activity in the etheric, has to do with the reawakening of the mysteries of the Divine Mother, which became suppressed with the coming of Christianity two thousand years ago. It came about that the mystery temple of Demeter, the Earth Mother, at Eleusis near Athens, and the other great mystery centers dedicated to the Divine Mother, such as the mystery center at Ephesus dedicated to Artemis, all became closed. The mysteries of the Mother were forgotten and suppressed. However, through the coming of the Etheric Christ, the mysteries of the Divine Mother are being opened once again.

This indicates to us something of the background of the widespread new interest in the Being of Mother Earth, in the sacred sites of Earth, beginning with the start of the New Age in 1899. The New Age, the Age of Light, could be called the Age of the Etheric Christ. As the preceding age, the age called in Hindu chronology Kali Yuga, the Dark Age, came to an end, a new Age of Light began. The Dark Age had extended over 5000 years, from the year 3102 B.C. extending up to the year 1899. Now we are living in the Age of Light extending over a period of 2500 years from 1899 until 4399, when there will come again a new impulse, that of the Astral Christ (Christ in the astral body) from 4399 onward.

If we look back 2000 years, we see that Christ came in a physical body and prepared the way for the coming Age of Pisces. Christ came toward the end of the Age of Aries. He was referred to by John the Baptist as the Lamb of God, the lamb or the ram, coming at the end of the Age of Aries. Yet his disciples were fishermen. He prepared the way for the coming of the Age of Pisces, which began in the year A.D. 215. This signified the end of the Age of Aries, and the beginning of the Age of Pisces. From this time onward, the early Christians began to use the symbol of the fish for Jesus.

With the Age of Pisces, humanity entered upon a path leading to materialism. This has to do with the fact that Pisces is connected with the feet. The feet are connected with the earth, and so through Pisces, we are most connected with the earth. What Christ brought was the spiritual side of Pisces, which is the impulse of love. The virtue of Pisces is: *"Magnanimity which becomes love."* Yet, without Christ, civilization has entered into materialism. Human beings are now anchored in the physical body. It was necessary for humanity to go through an age of being really anchored in the physical body. This development had to be for the sake of freedom—to be cut off from the spiritual, supersensible, and etheric worlds. Now, with the coming of the Etheric Christ, at this time at the end of the Age of Pisces, he is preparing for the Age of Aquarius.

Each age lasts for 2160 years, this being the length of time that the vernal point takes to pass through one sign of the zodiac. Thus the Age of Pisces extends up to the year 2375. Then the Age of Aquarius will begin, which will last for 2160 years, until the year 4535. Contemplating the Age of Light, this Age of the Etheric Christ, we can see clearly that the first part of the Age of Light coincides with the latter part of the Age of Pisces. Then from 2375 onward, the Age of Light coincides more or less with the Age of Aquarius. Thus we can divide the Age of Light into two parts: the first part, which is still in the Age of Pisces, and the second part, which more or less coincides with the Age of Aquarius. All of this was prophesied by Jesus Christ himself 2000 years ago in the Gospel of St. Matthew, chapter 24, when the disciples asked Jesus, *"What will be the sign of your Second Coming?"* He said: *"There will be wars, famine, earthquakes, and these will be but the beginning of the tribulation. There will be times of great tribulation. And then there will appear the sign of the Son of man in the heavens."* This is a reference to the entrance of the vernal point into Aquarius. How may this be understood?

The sign of Aquarius is that of the Waterbearer, depicted in the heavens pouring out water from an urn, streams of living water. What is the Waterbearer in relation to the human being? Actually, two-thirds of the human being is comprised of water. Analogously, Mother Earth is two-thirds water and one-third land. Each human being is one-third solid and two-thirds water, and in this two-thirds are the streaming forces of the etheric. Our life forces are borne by the Waterbearer in us. In this sense the Waterbearer is the etheric body. Just as Pisces has been an age of becoming anchored in the physical body and being aware only of the physical plane of existence, the Age of Aquarius will be a time of awakening to the etheric body and to the etheric plane of existence.

The work of the Etheric Christ now, in this last part of the Age of Pisces, is preparing the way, leading us into the Age of Aquarius. Through him it is possible to become aware of the etheric realm. Through Christ it is now possible, in the latter part of the Age of Pisces, to become clairvoyantly aware of the realm of the etheric, and to become aware of our own etheric body.

Regarding this, a tremendous battle is taking place. There are forces that would like to chain our consciousness to the physical body and to the physical plane of existence—forces opposing the work of the Etheric Christ in awakening us to the etheric level of existence. Thus an immense struggle is taking place, the outer signs of which are wars, earthquakes, and famines. This is the period of tribulation referred to by Christ in the Gospel of St. Matthew, a period of tribulation preceding the appearance of the sign of the Son of man in heaven, denoted by the entrance of the vernal point into Aquarius, the Waterbearer, the macrocosmic sign of the Etheric Christ. The tribulation is an expression of the battle taking place now between the forces of darkness that would like to chain us to the physical level of consciousness and the physical body, and the Etheric Christ, who is leading us to an awareness of the etheric plane of existence. Whether we use the word *tribulation* or the phrase *living in apocalyptic times*, these are times of a titanic conflict.

This provides a good background relating to the different ages. The work of the Etheric Christ is leading us now, during the last part of the Age of Pisces, into the Age of Aquarius, just as two thousand years ago at the end of the Age of Aries he prepared the way for the Age of Pisces. Here, I would like to focus upon the twentieth century and the time we are living in currently.

Looking at the 33 1/3-year rhythm of the etheric body of Christ, the most important time was the last 3 1/2 years, between the baptism in the Jordan and the Mystery of Golgotha. At the time of the baptism, the Christ Being descended and united with the physical vessel of Jesus. During this 3 1/2-year period following the baptism there was a raying in, a working in, of the Christ in his full power and majesty. He revealed himself through the signs and the miracles leading up to the greatest miracle, the Mystery of Golgotha, his death, sacrifice, and descent into the underworld, down toward the Kingdom of the Mother, and his resurrection and ascension to the Kingdom of the Father.

Now, since the start of the Light Age in 1899, following the unfolding of the 33 1/3-year rhythm of the Etheric Christ, we find three periods in the twentieth century demarcated by this rhythm. The first period, beginning in 1899, extends up to the year 1933. The most special period in this time was the last 3 1/2 years from 1929 to 1933. It was toward this period and the raying in of the Christ during this time that Rudolf Steiner's entire life's work was oriented. However, he died prematurely in 1925, shortly before the onset of the beginning of this first period of the raying in of the Christ during the first 33 1/3-year period of the Age of Light. It was during this time, as a manifestation of the counterforce directed against the coming of the Etheric Christ, that the forces of darkness focused upon one human being who, like Rudolf Steiner, came from Austria, and like Rudolf Steiner was active primarily in Germany—in the German-speaking world. Whereas Rudolf Steiner was an apostle of the Etheric Christ, this human being was a forerunner of the Antichrist. Through him was revealed a manifestation of the will of the Antichrist. He came to power in Germany in 1933, at exactly the time of the first culminating period of the activity of the Etheric Christ.

What was the Etheric Christ bringing in this period? It was an impulse toward *awakening the Divine I AM within*. The essence of this is summarized in the words of Paul: *"Not I, but Christ in me."* The Divine I AM is the true name of the Christ. When Christ is indwelling us, then we can truly say I AM. Then we are truly human beings.

The first phase of activity of the Etheric Christ in the Age of Light was to bring to birth the Divine I AM within. Everything in Anthroposophy leads to this. And since the essence of Anthroposophy is expressed in the Foundation Stone Meditation, it is not surprising to find in the Foundation Stone—in the fourth verse—that the hidden mantram is the I AM. This is what resounds through the last part of the Foundation Stone Meditation, the words I AM expressing the Divine I AM.

Let us now look at the second 33 1/3-year period in the twentieth century. In each period the unfolding of the work of the Etheric Christ presents a new aspect of his work. The second period culminated in the year 1966. The most important period in the time between 1933 and 1966 was the last 3 1/2 years, from 1962 to 1966. What was raying in as a special impulse of the Etheric Christ at this time? It was the impulse of community—community in Christ—the essence of which is expressed in the words, *"Where two or three are gathered together in my name, there am I in the midst of them."* Community in Christ is formed on the basis of the Divine I AM in individual human beings who come together in his name. It was the work of the Etheric Christ in this period of time to try and bring about the impulse toward community. Here again counterforces aligned to destroy this work of community-building—one example being the drug epidemic. It was the time when the drug prophets emerged. They preached drug-taking, signifying an impulse of dragging the human being down to become imprisoned in his own internal organism, which is the activity of drugs such as LSD. It was exactly at this time, when the impulse of Love and brotherhood was raying in, that the counterforce came about. The drug epidemic was only one manifestation of this counterforce; there are other aspects as well. Thus, the work of the Etheric Christ was countered during this particular period of time in the 1960s. And since then the counterforces have continued to work on.

Now we are in the third 33 1/3-year period leading up to the year 1999. The most special time in this third period is the culminating 3 1/2 years signifying a new raying in of the Etheric Christ. This 3 1/2-year period began in February 1996. Here a new level of activity of the Etheric Christ is coming to expression. What is apparent is a process of a step-by-step incarnation of the Etheric Christ: first in the individual as the Divine I AM, then in community as the power of Love building community, and now, the work of the Etheric Christ is beginning to manifest itself on a deeper level. This work is that of *redemption of the Divine Mother*. The work of the Etheric Christ in our time has to do with the pouring in of Divine Love into the kingdoms of Nature. Here again there is a counterforce at work, arising as an impulse to cut us off from the experience of Nature and to create an artificial world of counternature—a world totally removed from Nature. Whether we call it cyberspace, Internet, or virtual reality, we are referring to something that cuts us off from our divine, spiritual origin. Just at this time when the Etheric Christ is working to bring about a new relationship of humanity to the whole Earth as a Divine Being—a feeling for Mother Nature as a living spiritual Being with whom we are deeply connected—at this very time a most powerful impulse is sweeping across the planet drawing millions and millions of human beings into a world that is totally removed from Nature.

One aspect of the mystery of the coming of the Etheric Christ in the Age of Light is that just as 2000 years ago Christ Jesus lived through the three temptations in the wilderness on behalf of all humanity, now the whole of humanity is going through these three temptations in preparation for the unfolding of the true mission of humanity in the next millennium. The deeper reality of the encounter with the Etheric Christ will take place when we have passed through these three temptations. What are the three temptations?

The first is that of the *will to power*, the counterpart to the birth of the Divine I AM within. A most striking example of this was the ascent to power of the "Führer" in 1933. There it was a matter of one individual who manifested this will to power in an extraordinary way. He put himself forward as an outer authority in place of the true authority of the Divine I AM within.

The second period was the time when the second temptation really began to assert itself in relation to humanity. This is the temptation of *plunging from the pinnacle of the temple*. This signifies plunging down from our Divine I AM consciousness into the realm of the subconscious forces through drugs or alcohol, or through simply living out our instinctual life in an unbridled way, which is one way of plunging from the pinnacle of the temple. This was the temptation that humanity began to be confronted with on a large scale during the 1960s.

Now in the 1990s the third temptation is becoming increasingly active, that of *turning stones into bread*. This is the temptation of substituting the dead for the living. The world of virtual reality summarizes this perfectly. What's wrong with reality? Why do we have to substitute a virtual reality in place of reality? This is the substitution of stones for bread, the third temptation of humanity.

These temptations work in differing ways: the first temptation more on the level of the will, the second temptation on the level of the feeling life, and the third temptation on the level of the thought life. The third temptation is a more subtle temptation that appeals to our thinking faculty. These three temptations reveal to us the will, the feeling, and the thought life of the being who is called in Christian tradition the Antichrist—whom Rudolf Steiner calls Ahriman, and who is called in the Jewish tradition, Satan. It is also possible to speak of a fourth temptation: this is the *choice between Christ and Antichrist.* The fourth temptation is directed to the Self ("I") of the human being, just as the three temptations are directed toward the soul forces of willing, feeling, and thinking. Recollecting the emergence of Hitler in the 1930s, the manifestation of the will of Antichrist emerged then as something totally ruthless, a brutal will to destroy the sick, the needy, the weak. This has to do with the impulse that René called the animalizing of the body, as may be clearly seen from the image that was held up as the ideal in Nazi Germany, the image of the blonde beast, the intelligent beast who is fit, healthy, and ideally able to procreate a master human being on a physical level. The creation of the blonde beast may be seen as an archetype for the animalizing of the body.

Then there is the vegetabilizing of the soul, which is made possible through drugs, alcohol, and other such methods. A perfected form of this is apparent if we look at the treatment of psychiatric patients—the mentally ill—through psychotropic drugs. Anyone who sees what these drugs do knows they have a tendency to turn a human being into a walking vegetable, unable to think, feel, or truly act for him- or herself. However, any kind of drug-taking in the long term has the effect of vegetabilizing the soul.

Lastly, there is the mechanization of the spirit. This is the great temptation that is sweeping across humanity now—the mechanization of the spirit through the temptation of modern technology. To fall prey to this is to find that which modern technology offers more fascinating than the Divine Spirit. Through the activity of our own spirit, we can come into connection with Divine Wisdom. But now, as a substitute for this, instead of activating our own spirit, we can sit before a computer screen and tap into the knowledge of humanity through the Internet. This is a very wonderful tool, but it is also a great temptation to substitute this human knowledge for the Divine Wisdom, for the Divine Sophia. The temptation of turning stones into bread, leading to the mechanization of the human spirit, is now in full swing, taking place at this very time.

This temptation reveals the thought life of Antichrist, or Ahriman, who is casting his net to capture human souls, just as 2000 years ago Jesus Christ came and said to his disciples, *"Ye shall be fishers of men,"* in the sense of casting a net for the souls of human beings to become disciples of Christ. Now Antichrist is casting his net around the planet. These are apocalyptic times in which we are living, the times of tribulation prophesied by Jesus Christ when he said there would be war, earthquake, and famine. In 1906, shortly after the year 1899, the beginning of the New Age, there occurred the most powerful earthquake ever experienced in the United States—the great San Francisco earthquake. Since then there have been very many powerful earthquakes that have plagued the lives of thousands and thousands of people. We need only think of the 1923 Tokyo earthquake, which claimed the lives of 120,000 people.

Christ Jesus said it would be a time of earthquake, war, and famine. In 1914 World War I broke out and in 1939, shortly after, World War II—wars of a magnitude that had never been seen before upon this planet. It is estimated that so far in the twentieth century over 100 million people have died through war alone. And then there are the hundreds of thousands of starving human beings in third world countries; hundreds of thousands have died through famine. These are the times of tribulation referred to by Christ. This is the shadow side of the greatest event of our time, which is the coming of the Etheric Christ. And the coming of the Etheric Christ is now leading up to a great event in the year 1999.

Rudolf Steiner spoke of this in his lectures *From Jesus to Christ*, when he said that at the end of the twentieth century there will be a new Christ event on the etheric plane of existence. It will be a repetition of the Mystery of Golgotha, not on the physical plane, but in the etheric realm. This event will be as significant as the Mystery of Golgotha two thousand years ago. It has proved possible to exactly date this event. September 3-5, 1999, is the time of the repetition of the Mystery of Golgotha in the etheric. And 3 1/2 years prior to this, on February 23, 1996, was the repetition of the baptism in the Jordan on the etheric plane of existence. In my book, *Chronicle of the Living Christ*, I describe one possibility for following the activity of the Etheric Christ day by day, leading up to this great event in the history of the planet—the repetition of the Mystery of Golgotha in the etheric in September 1999. If we attune to this event we can begin to align ourselves with the daily increasing, strengthening, and radiating in of Divine Love, pouring into the etheric aura of the planet and permeating the whole of Nature. The whole Earth is becoming a Grail vessel with the Etheric Christ streaming in Divine Love. We can experience this love growing stronger and stronger day by day, as we proceed through the unfolding chronicle of the Living Christ—the Etheric Christ—to approach the great event at the end of the century. By becoming aware of these etheric occurrences, we can begin to take in the Christ's impulse to open up for us a path to the Divine Mother, a path toward experience of the Breath of Love emanating from the Kingdom of the Mother—Shamballa—and weaving through the whole of Nature.

So far, we have been looking at the three 33 1/3-year periods in the twentieth century relating to the temporal aspect of the mystery of the Etheric Christ, which is the other half of the mystery of Anthroposophy. Now I would like to draw attention to the spatial aspect of this mystery of the Etheric Christ. In each of these three periods, the Etheric Christ focuses on a particular geographic region. In the first period the focus was on Germany, or the German-speaking world. Why was this? In the German language, when one says the word "I," one says "ich," which is an abbreviation for—if you write it in Greek—*Iesous Christos*. The word *ich* in the German language actually signifies the Divine I AM, *Iesous Christos*, within. The German-speaking people, as Rudolf Steiner indicated, are the people who have a mission to bring this Divine I AM to birth. For this reason Anthroposophy, which has the task of leading to this birth of the Divine I AM, came into being in the German-speaking world through Rudolf Steiner, who came from Austria, was active in Germany, and founded the headquarters for the world anthroposophical movement in the German-speaking part of Switzerland. However, it was also in Germany that the counterimpulse to this birth of the Divine I AM within came about, culminating in the 1930s at the close of the first 33 1/3-year period.

A new focus for the raying in of the Etheric Christ developed during the second period, culminating in the 1960s. This was in the United

States. It was in the United States that the impulse to spiritual community arose most strongly, especially during the 1960s. Of course, it also spread to other parts of the world. From the first to the second 33 1/3-year period, a shift took place in the shining in of the Christ Sun, a shift from East to West, from Europe to America. Many of you will remember this, as this was taking place, especially on the West Coast, where there was a very strong raying in of this impulse of Love and community. It was also there that the counterimpulse arose most powerfully, with the drug epidemic that then spread across the world.

With the culmination of the third 33 1/3-year period, a further shift of the shining in of the Christ Sun is taking place—a shift westward to the realm of the Pacific, which is a very special area for the whole planet. William referred to the mountain chain extending from Alaska, down through the Rocky Mountains and through the Andes to the tip of South America, as the spinal column of Mother Earth. Rudolf Steiner spoke of Africa as the heart of Mother Earth and of the Pacific as the womb of Mother Earth. The Pacific is the most protected, intimate area of the planet. Into the womb of Mother Earth—the Pacific area—the Etheric Christ is now raying streams of life energy, life forces that weave across from the Pacific to the American continent and then across to the rest of the world. This follows the movement of the clouds. Those who study weather conditions will know that the Pacific is the most important area for the determination of the world's weather. If El Niño shifts a little, this has reverberations for the whole planet. The movements of the clouds from west to east give a picture of the streams of the working in of the Etheric Christ, now raying into the womb of Mother Earth, shining in new life, regenerating the planet. This working in is becoming stronger and stronger as we approach the end of this century, signifying a realization of the words from the first chapter of the Book of Revelation referring to the coming of the Etheric Christ *"in the clouds."*

Against this background we can see the task of Anthroposophy. As we approach the end of this century, leading up to the culminating event in September 1999, this event of the repetition of the Mystery of Golgotha in the etheric, a foundation stone for the unfolding of Christianity in the next millennium is being laid. The one side of this event we have been looking at today is the redemption of Mother Earth with the Etheric

Christ leading humanity along a path to the Divine Mother, opening the way to the Kingdom of the Mother, Shamballa. Anthroposophy prepares us for this event. The central task of Anthroposophy is to connect with this event of the Etheric Christ. The other side of the Christ event at the end of the twentieth century is the judgment of the living and the dead, with Christ becoming the Lord of Karma, thus forming a new relationship to every human being. However, the judgment is not taking place from without, but from within, through an awakening of conscience so that we begin to judge ourselves. This aspect of the Christ event at the end of the twentieth century is referred to by Rudolf Steiner in his lectures *From Jesus to Christ* (lecture of October 8, 1911). Thus, these are two sides of the great Christ event approaching at the end of the first century of the apocalyptic age, the Age of Light, the Age of the Etheric Christ.

Looking at the 33 1/3-year rhythm can help to give an orientation to a deeper understanding of the apocalyptic times in which we are living, and points to September 1999 as the culmination in the twentieth century of the activity of the Etheric Christ.

Great Signs from Heaven

In Christ's prophecy of his Second Coming he says:

> *Then will appear the sign of the Son of man in heaven, and then all the tribes of the earth will mourn, and they will see the Son of man coming on the clouds of heaven with power and great glory* (Matt. 24:30).

What is the "sign of the Son of man in heaven"? The three wise men from the East who bore gifts to pay homage to the newborn child Jesus were able to read the "sign of the Messiah in heaven" on the night of his birth. The three magi were the last representatives of the ancient star wisdom inaugurated by Zoroaster in Babylon in the sixth century B.C. As referred to already, Zoroaster may be credited with the primal intuition that led to the definition of the sidereal zodiac employed in the ancient star wisdom. Elsewhere I have described the intimate relationship between Zoroaster and the three magi and the child Jesus.[28]

In connection with Christ's prophecy, we are called upon to look up to the starry heavens and read the signs of his Second Coming, just as the three wise men read from the stars concerning his birth on Earth two thousand years ago. But whereas two thousand years ago it was a matter of the birth of Jesus Christ in a physical body, now the Son of man is coming on the "clouds of heaven," an expression that evokes the etheric realm of life forces. In other words, the Second Coming signifies the return of Christ in his etheric body into the biosphere surrounding the Earth as Nature's invisible matrix. To comprehend the Second Coming, we have to acquire an understanding of the life (etheric) body permeating the physical body and the realm to which it belongs—the etheric aura of Earth, which manifests itself in the biosphere.

The etheric body, visible to clairvoyant vision as an aura of light permeating the physical body, sustains the various rhythms—such as breathing and the beating of the heart—during the course of the human being's life on Earth. These discontinue at the moment of death when the etheric body separates from the physical, leaving the latter as a corpse. This radiant life body is also the bearer of memories. For, as many people who have had "near death experiences" have described, at the moment of death the human being experiences a panoramic flashback of his or her life. All memories accumulated during life suddenly well up as a tableau on account of the release of the etheric body from the physical. This is a result of the change in level of consciousness, with the human being now indwelling the etheric rather than the physical body. According to Rudolf Steiner's description, this experience of the "tableau of memories" inscribed in the etheric body lasts about three days, until the etheric body becomes reassimilated into the cosmic ether ("clouds of heaven").[29]

The human being continues to undergo very intense experiences in the life after death, and there begins a period of purification from earthly experiences. This is known in the East as kamaloca and in traditional Christian terminology as purgatory. It entails the reliving of everything experienced on Earth, in reverse order, in the light of moral conscience. It is an experience of judgment, actually self-judgment, through the awakening of conscience. This experience sets in shortly after death but generally remains obscured during the upheaval that takes place during the first forty days after death. The full awakening of conscience and experience of judgment thus begins about forty days after death. Some knowledge of the significance of these first forty days in the life after death has been preserved in the Orthodox Church, where it is customary to hold a memorial service for the departed soul after forty days. An archetype for this period of forty days is to be found in the life of the Risen One in the forty days from the resurrection to the ascension. During this period the Risen One remained in the Earth's aura and frequently appeared to the apostles and disciples. At the ascension he withdrew from Earth's aura into the angelic realm, as signified by the appearance of two Angels at the ascension (Acts 1:9). Following this archetype, there is a period of transition of forty days for every human being in the life after death, a crossing over from Earth's aura into the kingdom of the Angels, where the judgment proper (kamaloca/purgatory) then begins.

The fact that during the forty days after the resurrection the Risen One could appear as a definite manifestation to his disciples indicates that in his case, in contrast to the general course of events for most human beings, his etheric body did not dissolve back into the cosmos three days after death. Instead his etheric body, bearing all the memories of his life, remained intact and continued to be active following the Mystery of Golgotha. And it is this etheric body of Christ that is of special interest to us now, with his return in this body (rather than coming into incarnation in a physical body). An exact dating of the life of Jesus Christ shows that from birth to the Mystery of Golgotha was a period of exactly 33 1/3 years.[30]

Since the etheric body contains the entire biography, the rhythm of Christ's etheric body is 33 1/3 years. It is this rhythm (which may be likened to a planetary rhythm, e.g., the 29 1/2-year rhythm of Saturn's orbit around the sidereal zodiac) that holds the key to Christ's Second Coming, his return in his etheric body.

In the sense of being modern magi, looking to the cosmic signs of the return of the Son of man on the clouds of heaven, we may follow the 33 1/3-year rhythm as a kind of (invisible) planetary rhythm in history. Following the ascension in A.D. 33, Christ's etheric body expanded into the cosmos, reaching the outermost boundary of the etheric cosmos after twenty-eight 33 1/3-year cycles in the year 966, which signified a turning point. Then began a contraction and descent—a return toward Earth—of this etheric body, again through twenty-eight 33 1/3-year cycles, returning to Earth's etheric aura in 1899. The return of Christ was prophesied by the Angels at the ascension in the words: "Men of Galilee, why do you stand looking into heaven? This Jesus, who was taken up from you into heaven, will come in the same way as you saw him go into heaven" (Acts 1:11).

The year 1899 thus marked a very decisive turning point in history, the end of an age (known in the East as Kali Yuga, the Dark Age) and the start of a New Age, the Age of Light. The transition that began in 1899, affecting the entire Earth, can be likened to a kind of death experience, the beginning of a separation between the physical body and the etheric body of the Earth. And just as the life of the human soul after death may be followed through various stages, so may the New Age of the Earth since 1899 be followed. But before we do so, it will help to clarify the term "New Age" especially as it is a term that is now in popular usage.

It seems that Rudolf Steiner was the first person to use the term "New Age", and he did so in the context of his lectures on the true nature of the Second Coming.[31] This event has to do with the return of Christ in his etheric body into Earth's etheric aura, an occurrence that may be dated to the year 1899. The New Age that began in 1899/1900 could be called the Age of the Second Coming. However, since the first 33 1/3-year period of this New Age was a time of reincorporation of Christ's etheric body into Earth's etheric aura, in a certain sense the Age of the Second Coming began for humanity in 1933. This was the date indicated by Rudolf Steiner for the start of a new kind of etheric clairvoyance with which Christ's Second Coming is able to be perceived.[32] To use an analogy, 1899 could be termed the "dawn" of the New Age and 1933 the "sunrise," when the Sun of Righteousness, Jesus Christ, began to become visible to human beings again in the same way as he manifested himself to the apostles and disciples during the forty days from the resurrection to the ascension.

It is clear, therefore, that the New Age is not to be identified with the Age of Aquarius, as is commonly done. The "New Age" movement that has arisen in the twentieth century is right in proclaiming that a New Age has begun, but it is a mistake to identify this with the zodiacal Age of Aquarius, which will not commence until the year 2375. Nevertheless, the New Age—that of Christ's Second Coming— leads humanity into the Aquarian Age. And it is this relationship of the New Age to the Aquarian Age to which we shall now turn our attention, with the help of this analogy between the human being's life after death and the process of separation between the physical and etheric that is taking place (since 1899) for the Earth as a whole.

In contemplating the human being's life after death, the first three days are taken up with the beholding of the tableau of memories of the biography that unfolded between birth and death. With regard to Christ's Second Coming, what are the "days"? For the human being the daily rhythm of day and night is the rhythm of the self ("I"), the week is the rhythm of the astral body, and the month is the rhythm of the etheric body.[33] For Christ, as I have discussed earlier in this book, the 12-year Jupiter rhythm is the rhythm of the Christ Self, the 29 1/2-year Saturn period is the rhythm of Christ's astral body, and the 33 1/3-year rhythm is that of Christ's etheric body. Therefore it is the 12-year Jupiter rhythm that is relevant to the unfolding of the days of "world judgment" that began with the twentieth century, or rather with the last Full Moon of the nineteenth century. This took place on December 17, 1899, on which day the Sun and Saturn entered into conjunction with one another. On this day Jupiter (heliocentrically) entered sidereal Scorpio, from which point in time we can follow the "days" of Christ in the orbits of Jupiter around the sidereal zodiac. (Here it would lead too far from our theme to discuss the deeper significance of heliocentric Jupiter's entrance into sidereal Scorpio.) The exact sidereal period of Jupiter's orbit of the zodiac is 11.86 years. Taking each orbit to be one "day," three "days" amount to 35 1/2 years.

In terms of applying an analogy between the first three days after the human being's death and the first three "days" of the New Age, we find that these "days" extend from the end of 1899 up to the middle of the year 1935 (an important date also mentioned by Rudolf Steiner in connection with the Second Coming—see endnote 32). With regard to this "death experience" for the Earth as a whole, with the beginning in 1899/1900 of the separation of the Earth's etheric aura from the physical Earth, those three "days" were a time of a panoramic flashback of the history of the Earth as a whole. Something of this we find embodied in Rudolf Steiner's Anthroposophy, which came into being during this time, and which contains an outline of the entire spiritual history of the Earth with the Mystery of Golgotha as the pivotal center. The birth of Anthroposophy in the years 1900 to 1925, the year of Rudolf Steiner's death, can thus be seen to stand in direct relationship to Christ's Second Coming.

How does this analogy of "days" in the New Age apply when we look at the forty days of upheaval following death, leading to the start of kamaloca proper, with the human being's entrance into the realm of the Angels approximately forty days after death? Forty Jupiter "days" amount to 474 1/2 years (= 40 x 11.86). Adding this to 1900, we arrive at the year 2374. And as already referred to, the zodiacal Age of Aquarius commences in 2375. In this sense the New Age leads into the Aquarian Age. The forty "days" of upheaval from 1900 to 2374 comprise the period of tribulation referred to by Christ in prophesying his Second Coming (Matt. 24:3-28). "Immediately after the tribulation of those days . . . the powers of the heavens will be shaken; then will appear the sign of the Son of man in heaven" (Matt. 24:29-30). With the entrance of the vernal point into Aquarius, "he will send out his Angels" (Matt.24:31), corresponding to the human being's entrance into the realm of the Angels forty days after death.

In the spirit of the magi who beheld the sign of the Messiah in heaven on the night of his birth, we have attempted here to decipher the "sign of the Son of man in heaven" relating to Christ's Second Coming. This requires a knowledge of the rhythms of the different members of Christ's being, such as the 33 1/3-year rhythm of his etheric body and the 12-year Jupiter rhythm of Christ's Self. This in turn leads us to an understanding of the New Age as the Age of the Second Coming, leading into the zodiacal Age of Aquarius. The entrance of the vernal point into sidereal Aquarius is the "sign of the Son of man in heaven." Aquarius is the Waterman, and the "waterman" within the human being is the fluidic etheric body (as opposed to the solid physical body). In looking up to the sidereal sign of Aquarius in the heavens, an image of the Risen One in his etheric body is evoked, pouring forth the living water, "a spring of water welling up to eternal life" (John 4:14). It is here that we see the relationship between the New Age —understood in its true sense—and the zodiacal Age of Aquarius.

Identifying the New Age as the Age of the Second Coming, let us now look more closely at the first part of the New Age and to the stages of incarnation of the Etheric Christ. In response to the inquiry on the part of the disciples concerning his Second Coming, Jesus Christ spoke of wars, earthquakes, famines, pestilence, and "great signs from heaven" (Luke 21:11). The New Age of the Second Coming began in 1899, according to Rudolf Steiner's dating. It is characterized by the 33 1/3-year rhythm of the life of Jesus Christ, whereby it is always the last 3 1/2 years of each 33 1/3-year period that are of particular significance.[34] These special 3 1/2-year periods of the Etheric Christ in the twentieth century were/are: (1) June 29, 1929 - January 8, 1933; (2) October 27, 1962 - May 9, 1966; and (3)

February 24, 1996 - September 6, 1999. In each case it is a matter of the renewed activity of the Etheric Christ, at the same time countered by forces of opposition. These periods are focal points in time, which does not mean to say that the Etheric Christ and the forces of opposition are not also active at other times as well.

Period (3) is the most significant of the three, as it signifies a culmination of the activity of the Etheric Christ, now active on the level of the will, having "incarnated" through the levels of (1) thought and (2) feeling. The significance of (3), especially the end of this period in September 1999, was referred to by Rudolf Steiner already in 1911:

> Just as on the physical plane in Palestine, at the beginning of our era, an event occurred in which the most important part was taken by Christ himself, an event which has significance for the whole of humanity, so in the course of the twentieth century, towards the end of the twentieth century, a significant event will again take place, not in the physical world, but in the world we usually call the world of the etheric. And this event will have as fundamental a significance for the evolution of humanity as the event of Palestine had at the beginning of our era.[35]

The significance of period (3)—denoting a reliving in the etheric of the 3 1/2-year ministry of Christ—was highlighted by the appearance of the comet Hyakutake announcing the start (in late February 1996) of these 3 1/2 years at the end of the twentieth century. This was the first sign in the heavens. The second sign was the appearance exactly one year later of the Comet Hale-Bopp announcing the beginning (in late February 1997) of the second year of the 3 1/2 years of ministry of the Etheric Christ. And the third sign was the total solar eclipse on February 26, 1998, announcing the commencement of the third year of the Etheric Christ's ministry.

The positive significance of this eclipse is that it denotes an intensification of the entrance into the etheric of Christ, whose work now is for the redemption of Mother Earth. Just as when Jesus Christ entered the city of Jerusalem two thousand years ago—at which time (on March 19, A.D. 33) there was an eclipse of the Sun (not visible in Jerusalem)—so now with the eclipse on February 26, 1998, this can be seen as an important stage on the path of the Etheric Christ entering into the domain of the New Jerusalem and establishing his kingdom: "a new heaven and a new earth" (Rev. 21:1). With this, heavenly forces are descending from above, and through the work of the Etheric Christ in transforming the Earth, a New Earth is coming into being. Consequently, Mother Earth is undergoing birth pangs, and with each new contraction there is more of an opening and a release from the depths of something that was—until now (in a certain respect)—both hidden from the rays of the Sun and also not reached by the light and warmth of the Sun of Righteousness. So it is that during the course of the twentieth century definite manifestations of evil have arisen and continue to arise from the abyss. In period (1) it was especially the will of Antichrist that arose from the abyss in the shape of the Nazi beast. (The expression "Antichrist" is used here to denote a personification of the force—or forces—of opposition to the Etheric Christ.) In period (2) the feeling life of Antichrist manifested itself in various ways, particularly in the surfacing of the drug culture. And in period (3) the thought life of Antichrist is now becoming revealed, one example of which is the emergence of cyberspace, a thought-realm far removed from divine reality. (Cyberspace is mentioned here only as one aspect of a whole complex of related phenomena.) Of course, cyberspace in itself is not evil, no more than drugs are. And just as there is a right clinical/medical use of drugs, so there is also a right use of cyberspace. The "how" of this right use is the all-important question.

Returning to the total solar eclipse of February 26, 1998 (actually the following remarks apply to all solar eclipses):

> (a) the time of the darkening of the Sun's rays is a time when certain negative aspects of existence may come forth; and (b) the eclipsing of the Sun's forces can call forth in human beings their own inner Sun forces, having to do especially with the will. Out of human free will what needs to be called forth is gratitude for the mysteries of the Sun, which are essentially threefold:
>
> (1) The Sun is not only the source of light, life, and warmth but is also the outer manifestation of the kingdom of heaven, a place of abode of sublime spiritual beings;

(2) the Sun itself is a visible expression of the Son of God, the Christ Mystery;

(3) the Sun points us toward the "Son of man," the Etheric Christ, who is working to open the heart chakra in human beings (the heart is the center of the human being corresponding to the Sun at the heart of the solar system) and who may be visualized as a radiant Sun now at work within the Earth's biosphere.

Indeed, at the time of a solar eclipse it is always appropriate to hold in consciousness the image of Jesus Christ's triumphant entry into Jerusalem, since this event took place historically on the day of a solar eclipse. In so doing, the most important qualities to be cultivated, which the Etheric Christ can connect with, are reverence, compassion, and conscience: reverence for the divine mystery of existence in all its aspects; compassion for Mother Earth and for all the beings connected with her, all seeking redemption; and heightened conscience as a sense of vigilance for the good. Vigilant conscience is especially important at the time of a solar eclipse, because when the warmth and light of the Sun are blotted out, cold and dark forces may try to gain entrance into human consciousness. Hence the importance of taking hold of one's own inner Sun, which like the outer Sun is always burning and aflame, and is darkened only when conscience is lulled to sleep.

The question is: What was special about the solar eclipse of February 26, 1998? Was it not just another solar eclipse, like every other one? What made it special is the timing of it in relation to the 3 1/2 years of the Etheric Christ's ministry. It belongs to a different order of time. It is because it is the third sign, after Hyakutake and Hale-Bopp (heavenly signs that also deserved our attention, awe, and wonder), signifying an opening to Divine Love. In a certain respect it is the greatest of the three signs, just as Love is greater than faith (the quality called forth by Hyakutake) and hope (the quality called forth by Hale-Bopp). With this solar eclipse there began to flow in a great teaching about Divine Love as the foundation of all existence, a teaching directed to hearts that are open. Moreover, Mother Earth is opening to receive this gift of Divine Love, and we are called upon to feel warmth and compassion for Mother Earth as she opens herself and goes through her birth pangs of transformation through the work of the Etheric Christ. In the wake of the eclipse, in the time following, many things will be uncovered and discovered, seen and understood, sensed and felt concerning the mystery of Divine Love.

This is the positive side, which has to do with the preparation for the great Christ event in September 1999, referred to—not explicitly, but implicitly—in the above quote by Rudolf Steiner. A significant moment in time on the way toward this event is the commemoration—see *The Chronicle of The Living Christ*[36]—of the raising of Lazarus. Historically this event took place on Saturday, July 26 A.D. 32. In the current ministry of the Etheric Christ—period (3)—this event was relived in the etheric world at Christmas 1998. This is followed by the total solar eclipse on August 11, 1999, falling within a few days (in the chronicle of the Etheric Christ) of the commemoration of the triumphant entry of Jesus Christ into Jerusalem. Moreover, this is the last total solar eclipse of the twentieth century, and on account of the path of visibility of its totality (across France, Germany, and Austria) it is called the "European eclipse." Similar remarks apply to this total solar eclipse as to the one on February 26, 1998, with the additional significance that the total solar eclipse of August 11, 1999, more or less coincides in the chronicle of the Etheric Christ with the triumphant entry of Jesus into Jerusalem. In other words, it is a real expression of this event in the etheric, and is not simply a cosmic remembrance of the historical event. The solar eclipse on August 11, 1999, shortly precedes the culminating Golgotha event—the Mystery of Golgotha in the etheric [September 3-5, 1999]—in this last period of renewed activity of the Etheric Christ in the twentieth century. This signifies a Grail event for the whole Earth: an inpouring of Divine Love with the entire Earth being a Grail vessel to receive this inflow. If nothing else, one purpose of this book is to draw attention to this event, which "will have as fundamental a significance for the evolution of humanity as the event of Palestine had at the beginning of our era" (Rudolf Steiner).

This event signifies the laying of a Foundation Stone for at least the next two thousand years of Christianity, as the Mystery of Golgotha laid the Foundation Stone for the past two thousand years. This event—setting the Earth and humanity on the right course for the future—is the primary event of our time, which, however, is being countered by the secondary event of the incarnation of the Antichrist, who is seeking to divert the Earth and humanity from the proper course of evolution. In the Judeo-Christian tradition the Antichrist is generally identified as Satan. Yet it is also illuminating to consider the ancient Persian tradition that refers to Satan as Ahriman. In the Zoroastrian (Persian) tradition Ahriman is described as the evil twin of Ahura Mazdao, who is easily recognizable as a pre-Christian (pre-incarnatory) form of Christ. Similarly, Ahriman is readily recognizable as Satan.

The ancient Zoroastrian texts describe how Ahriman issued a challenge to Ahura Mazdao, saying that he would win over all those belonging to Ahura Mazdao, all the human souls (likened to hosts of shining stars in the firmament). Ahura Mazdao accepts the challenge, but sets a time limit upon the period of confrontation. If we interpret this as applying to the conflict between Christ (Ahura Mazdao) and Satan (Ahriman), then it would seem that the deadline set by this time limit is approaching soon. Obviously, as the climax to the confrontation, the incarnation of Ahriman has to take place before this deadline, which in the chapter "The Second Coming and the Approaching Trial of Humanity" is indicated to be the year 2047. Rudolf Steiner's statement that the incarnation of Ahriman is to take place shortly after the start of the third millennium sheds light upon the spiritual background to the present world situation, at least according to this interpretation.

From this standpoint there is evidently—outwardly—feverish preparation taking place for the incarnation of Ahriman, the prince of darkness; inwardly the Grail event connected with Christ's Second Coming is being prepared for. This means that there is a battle of apocalyptic dimensions now taking place—a battle upon which the future of the Earth and humanity depends. This battle is being waged through human beings, who often are oblivious to the fact that they are pawns in a titanic struggle; and if they are unwittingly working to further the aims of the prince of darkness, the appropriate words are: Father, forgive them, for they know not what they do. Indeed, how can they know what they do, without having some spiritual frame of reference?

The Apocalypse, as described in the Book of Revelation, does give a frame of reference, if its images can be interpreted in the right way as depicting a prophetic view of history. Yet, how is it possible to make a start in interpreting the mighty images of the Apocalypse? Thanks to

Rudolf Steiner, one very concrete time indication was given that applies to chapter 12 of the Book of Revelation. The passage in question follows after the great sign in heaven referring to Divine Sophia, "A woman clothed with the Sun, with the Moon under her feet, and on her head a crown of twelve stars" (Rev. 12:1):

> *Now war arose in heaven, Michael and his angels fighting against the dragon; and the dragon and his angels fought, but they were defeated and there was no longer any place for them in heaven. And the great dragon was thrown down, that ancient serpent, who is called the Devil and Satan, the deceiver of the whole world—he was thrown down to the earth, and his angels were thrown down with him* (Rev. 12:7-9).

In his lectures *The Fall of the Spirits of Darkness*, Rudolf Steiner describes how the war in heaven lasted about forty years, culminating in the year 1879 with the start of a new Age of Michael. If this date is taken together with the start of the New Age of the Second Coming in 1899, a comprehensive understanding of the images in chapter 12 of the Book of Revelation becomes possible. It appears that Divine Sophia emerged to "give birth." That is, just as Jesus was born of Mary two thousand years ago, now on a cosmic level, Divine Wisdom prepares for the birth of the Etheric Christ. Rudolf Steiner's mission as the founder of Anthroposophia, which can be regarded as a modern offspring of Divine Sophia, was to prepare the way for the approaching birth of the Etheric Christ (a birth of Christ into the etheric world). In this he was assisted by the Archangel Michael.

There is an indirect confirmation of Rudolf Steiner's dating of the "war in heaven" to the 40-year period culminating in 1879. Immediately prior to describing the war in heaven, chapter 12 of Revelation depicts the emergence of the "great sign in heaven" relating to Divine Sophia. Divine Sophia is the bearer of the heavenly forces descending from above, as the Bride of the Lamb bringing the "new heaven" to unite with the "new earth" created by the Lamb, according to chapter 21 of the Book of Revelation. Divine Sophia has essentially been holding back with her contribution to world evolution, waiting for the right moment in time to start bringing down the heavenly forces from above. Thus, in Dante's vision—in "Paradise," the third part of his *Divine Comedy*—he describes the Celestial Rose in the Empyreum, the highest heaven. Dante wrote the *Divine Comedy* in the early part of the fourteenth century (he died in 1321).

According to the Russian visionary mystic and prophet of the Eternal Feminine, Daniel Andreev (1906-1959), Divine Sophia—seen in his visions in relation to the "Rose of the World"– had begun her descent from the highest heaven already by the beginning of the nineteenth century. Andreev saw that at this point in time there began the incarnation of Divine Sophia, a descent culminating with a birth in the etheric "in a body of enlightened ether," leading to the founding of the "Rose of the World" as a new world culture of the Divine Feminine. This he describes in his book *The Rose of the World*:

> Since ancient times the loftiest hearts and subtlest minds have anticipated this event that is now taking place. The first link in the chain of events—events so important that they can only be compared to the incarnation of the Planetary Logos—occurred at the turn of the nineteenth century. This was the emanation of the energy of the Virgin Mother, an emanation that was not amorphous, as it had been twice before in human history, but incomparably intensified by the personal aspect it assumed. A great God-born monad descended from the heights of the Universe into Shadanakar. Almost a century later, Vladimir Soloviev was given a glimpse of Raoris—one of the highest planes in our bramfatura, which She had entered—when, on a starry night in the Egyptian desert, he experienced a stunning breach of his consciousness and saw the Great Feminine Being with his own eyes. Zventa-Sventana we call Her, She Who is the Brightest and All-Good, the expression of the Feminine Hypostasis of the Trinity. She now abides in Bayushmi, one of the regions that are part of the sakwala of the Waves of World Femininity. The long-awaited day approaches when She will descend to one of the great cities in the metacultures. There She is to be born in a body of enlightened ether, the child of a demiurge and one of the Great Sisters. A host of the loftiest souls from the Elite of Shadanakar will descend with Her into that zatomis. There She is, our hope and joy, Light and

> Divine Beauty! For Her birth will be mirrored in our history as something that our grandchildren and great-grandchildren will witness: the founding of the Rose of the World, its spread throughout the world, and, if a terrible human blunder does not hurl us down into the depth of darkness, the assumption by the Rose of the World of supreme authority over the entire Earth.[37]

Andreev's vision can be viewed against the background of the emergence of Divine Sophia as the *"great sign in heaven"* in chapter 12 of the Book of Revelation. In the light of Andreev's description, the start of chapter 12—the appearance of Divine Sophia—began "at the turn of the nineteenth century," i.e. close in time to the death in 1801 of the young German romantic poet Novalis, who was also inspired by Divine Sophia as is evident from his *Spiritual Songs* and *Hymns To the Night*. Some forty years later the war in heaven followed, according to Rudolf Steiner, in the period from 1841 to 1879. Additional confirmation of this dating is provided by the phenomenon of apparitions of the Virgin Mary. Thomas Schipflinger, in his book *Sophia-Maria,* traces the relationship between Sophia and the Virgin Mary.[38] Given this relationship, it is not surprising to find that—synchronizing with the beginning of the descent of Divine Sophia in the nineteenth century—the new series of apparitions of the Virgin Mary began with her appearance in Paris to the Catholic nun Catherine Labouré in 1830. This was followed by apparitions in 1846 (La Salette), 1858 (Lourdes), 1917 (Fatima), and 1981 (Medjugorje)—to name a few of the most famous ones.

Almost all accounts of the apparitions of the Virgin Mary indicate the 1830 appearances in Paris as the start of the series of "modern apparitions."[39] Of course, there were reports of earlier apparitions, yet the Paris vision (1830) and certain subsequent ones—especially La Salette (1846), Lourdes (1858), and Fatima (1917)—were each approved by the local bishop and have since gained international attention. In light of the dating of the emergence of Divine Sophia as the *"great sign in heaven"* (Rev. 12:1), 1830 fits well with Daniel Andreev's and Rudolf Steiner's indications. Accepting this apocalyptic scenario as a working hypothesis, the question arises as to how subsequent events fit in. Thus, *"when the dragon saw that he had been thrown down to the earth, he pursued the woman"* (Rev.

12:13). Or, as stated a few verses later: *"Then the dragon was angry with the woman, and went off to make war on the rest of her offspring. . . ."* (Rev. 12:17).

This quotation could refer to various events in our time. In the light of the foregoing it bears an obvious relationship with the ascent of the Nazi beast and the consequence thereof: World War II. As discussed in the foregoing, the Nazi beast was a manifestation of the will of Antichrist (Ahriman, Satan, or the dragon). Since the work of Rudolf Steiner, who was a servant of the Divine Sophia and the Etheric Christ, took root primarily in Germany (note that Rudolf Steiner was Austrian), the counter-impulse (focused through another Austrian) also struck back in Germany with extraordinary force.

This interpretation admittedly centers upon only one aspect of the image of the dragon waging war. (Another aspect that we could consider, although going into detail concerning it would lead too far afield, is the reign of communism that struck against the impulse of Divine Sophia in Russia: bear in mind the significance of Vladimir Soloviev, founder of Russian Sophiology, as an emissary of Divine Sophia for the Russian people.) If we accept this interpretation, we can look back over the course of the twentieth century and find dramatic evidence that the "dragon waging war" is a ferocious thing indeed. However, this recent history is only preparatory for what then follows in chapter 13 of the Book of Revelation: *"Men worshipped the dragon, for he had given his authority to the beast . . . and it was allowed to exercise authority for forty-two months"* (Rev. 13:4-5).

What is meant by the dragon giving his authority to the beast? One possible way of understanding this is in relation to the incarnation of the dragon. That is, the beast may be regarded as the incarnated dragon, i.e., the incarnation of Ahriman. It is this act of incarnation, in the light of this interpretation, that is signified by the words "giving authority." Ahriman or Satan (the dragon), after waging war on the offspring of Divine Sophia and *"those who bear testimony to Jesus"* (Rev. 12:17), then incarnates. As the beast, he is allowed to rule the Earth (*"exercise authority"*) for forty-two months, i.e., for 3 1/2 years, corresponding to the period on Earth of the ministry of Jesus Christ. In this interpretation the beast is identical with the Antichrist of Christian tradition. If this is true, there still remains the question: When will this 3 1/2-year period of rulership of the Antichrist take place?

In answering this question, in his lectures *The Influences of Lucifer and Ahriman,* Rudolf Steiner uses the expression—in referring to the incarnation of Ahriman as a human being—"not long after the start of the third millennium." This could mean just a few years or some longer period of time. Earlier in this book the perspective is given that the human being who is to become the vehicle for Ahriman (analogous to Jesus, who became the vessel for the Christ) was born in 1962, and that the incarnation of Ahriman could take place around the year 2010. If this interpretation is correct, the human being in question will be about forty-eight years old, and would thus conceivably be in a position to become world ruler for a period of 3 1/2 years. Treating this as a hypothesis, we should be able to look for phenomena that would either confirm or refute this interpretation. However, this means taking a closer look at chapter 13 of the Book of Revelation: *"And authority was given it [the beast] over every tribe and people and tongue and nation . . ."* (Rev. 13:7). This points to a global rulership. In this respect the setting up of a global communications network appears in a new light. And it would also explain the speed with which this is proceeding: the need to have everything in place in time for the emergence of the beast (Antichrist, in the Christian tradition, or Ahriman, in Rudolf Steiner's terminology).

Also important here is the reference in chapter 13 to the two-horned beast that *"makes the earth and its inhabitants worship the first beast"* (Rev. 13:12). In the earlier chapter of this book, "The Second Coming and the Approaching Trial of Humanity," reference was made to the two-horned beast, whose number is 666, as having to do with the prophet of the Antichrist. Analogous to John the Baptist, the prophet who prepared the way for the coming of Christ, this prophet will prepare the way for the incarnation of Ahriman. This prophet will be a vehicle for the inspiration of the so-called "Sun Demon" (Sorath), whose number is 666, as described earlier. And 1998 (= 3 x 666) might well be the year in which the prophet begins his work, a work that would extend through one Jupiter cycle of twelve years, until the incarnation of Ahriman (Satan) in a human being takes place.

One of the signs of the prophet is that of *"making fire come down from heaven"* (Rev. 13:13). Is it not striking that this is one of the goals of HAARP (High-frequency Active Auroral Research Project)? HAARP is a military research project located in Alaska.[40] One of its goals is to harness the electrical forces of the ionosphere (that manifest themselves, for example, in the aurora borealis, the northern lights), and to call these forces down from heaven. The intention is to have HAARP operational in 1998. The goal of HAARP could be said to be *"making fire come down from heaven,"* a kind of calling down of lightning. Whoever would control such a facility would then be able to *"deceive those who dwell on earth, bidding them make an image for the beast . . . "* (Rev. 13:14).

At this juncture it is interesting to consider the thunderbird of the North American Indians. The thunderbird for them is a personification of the electrical forces at work in Earth's upper atmosphere. The northern lights, for example, proceed from the "mouth of the thunderbird." And, according to Indian prophecy, the white race would one day try to harness the thunderbird—but, according to prophecy, this would cause a violent reaction on the part of Mother Earth. Such an image can be taken as a warning not to interfere with the Earth's subtle organism, that to do so could have dire consequences. In other words, Mother Earth needs to be seen and experienced—as the Native American Indians do—as a living being, whose aura encompasses the ionosphere as part of her subtle body, which should not be interfered with.

Another interesting Native American prophecy, this time on the part of the Hopi Indians, concerns the iron spider. The Hopi prophecy refers to the creation—on the part of the white race—of an "iron spider" to put Mother Earth in chains. Again, according to this prophecy, this would result in catastrophe, because Mother Earth would not stand for it. This prophecy could be interpreted as relating to the grid of satellites around the Earth planned to facilitate the global communications network. Again, it is a warning that Mother Earth will not stand for this endeavor to put her in bondage and cut her off from the cosmos. Yet this is the intention of Ahriman (Satan), to cut the Earth off from the cosmos and divert the evolution of the Earth and humanity in another direction than that intended by Christ and Sophia.

The satellites making up the "iron spider" are all part of the global communications network, which functions by way of images (TV screen or computer screen). Could this be what the "making an image" refers to in Revelation 13:14? *"Worship of the image of the beast"* (Rev. 13:15) might signify submitting oneself to the influence of Antichrist, who would control the global communications network and rule the world via the images appearing on the screen (including images of himself, of course). It is interesting to consider the message of the comets Hyakutake and Hale-Bopp in this light. What an extraordinary appearance was presented to us in the night sky during the first part of 1997 by the comet Hale-Bopp! Who was not moved at the sight of its radiance and its sweeping tail? How many followed its path as it traversed the starry heavens? What was the message of this comet? Was it proclaiming a blessing? Or was it issuing a warning to humanity?

In order to begin to answer these questions, we have to start to learn to read the starry script. This is something that 99 percent of the astronomers around the world have stopped doing. And astrologers, for the most part—at least, in the West—no longer refer to the actual world of stars. Yet perhaps the appearance of Hale-Bopp might have helped to awaken some to the reality of the starry heavens? Seeing the comet pass along above the stretched out (lying down) figure of Andromeda and just beneath the star Algol, which marks the "evil eye" in the head of Medusa carried by the hero Perseus, the question could arise: What is the starry script communicating to us here?

That an actual message was being addressed to humanity from the heavens becomes clear if we also take into consideration the comet Hyakutake, which put in an appearance as a bright comet exactly one year prior to Hale-Bopp. The very occurrence of two powerful comets in successive years at the end of the twentieth century is in itself something quite extraordinary, in view of the fact that there have been hardly any bright comets visible at all this century. But when considered in relation to the 3 1/2-year period of the Parousia of Christ—his appearance in spiritual form—at the end of the twentieth century, the coincidence is very striking indeed.

According to research referred to earlier, this period began on February 23, 1996 (recalling the baptism), and extends to September 3-5,

1999 (remembering the Mystery of Golgotha). The start of this period toward the end of February 1996 coincided with the coming of Hyakutake, which became visible to the naked eye during March 1996. One year later, the appearance of Hale-Bopp also visible to the naked eye proclaimed the beginning of the second year of this 3 1/2-year period of recollection of Christ's ministry. This conviction is based on observation and meditation on the meaning and significance of the two comets. The appearance of these two comets can be seen in the light of Christ's words concerning "great signs from heaven" (Luke 21:11), when he was asked by his disciples about his return. [Note that the Greek word *Parousia*, meaning "presence," indicates the spiritual nature of Christ's return, as a presence in the Earth's biosphere—"in the clouds" (Rev. 1:7)—and not in a physical form.] In this light, Hyakutake and Hale-Bopp have been proclaiming a blessing upon humanity, announcing the renewed presence of Christ during this special 3 1/2-year period at the end of the twentieth century.

At the same time, however, the comets have been issuing a warning. This is expressed in the extraordinary fact that the paths of the two comets intersected at the star Algol exactly one year apart in time: Hyakutake traversed Algol on April 11, 1996 and Hale-Bopp passed just below Algol exactly one year later, on the night of April 10/11, 1997. The probability of this being mere coincidence is very small indeed. The question is (in terms of reading the starry script): What does Algol signify? For the ancients it marked the evil eye. It symbolized the decadent power of the ancient clairvoyance, represented by the Medusa, which had to make way for the new faculty of intelligence represented by Perseus. Using his intelligence he was able to slay the Medusa and rescue Andromeda, symbolizing the soul of humanity.

Since the birth of philosophy in the days of ancient Greece, to which the Perseus myth refers, intelligence has developed: theology, advanced mathematics, celestial mechanics and other sciences, and also technology have come into being through the development of the faculty of human intelligence. But now with the computer revolution, intelligence is in danger of becoming mechanized. The mechanization of intelligence would signify the "end of the line" for the development of human thinking. And this is the danger to which the comets are drawing attention, if we learn to read the starry script.

In my view the new "evil eye" in our time is the computer screen (or the television screen). Millions of people sit motionless for hours on end in front of a screen that seems to exert a hypnotic influence upon them. Just as in ancient times the gaze of the Medusa turned to stone all who beheld it, so this modern evil eye also "turns to stone" (hypnotizes and reduces movement to a minimum). It would seem, therefore, that the deeper message of the comets is to warn about the danger of a new "evil eye" while at the same time pointing to the next stage of human thought-life beyond philosophy, science, and technology, where thinking may become seeing. A new clairvoyance is to arise, through which Christ (as the Parousia) may be seen or felt as a presence in the Earth's biosphere ("in the clouds"). In line with this it seems that the comets are helping in the development of new organs of perception, arising through living thinking rather than mechanized thinking, a thinking that is able to become a seeing, to behold Christ in spiritual form. Thus, these two comets may be seen as Divine Messengers from on high, speaking out— or actually radiating out— Divine Wisdom to help humankind forward at this special (and difficult) time in the evolution of humanity and the Earth. As referred to earlier, Hyakutake brought a faith-renewing impulse, and Hale-Bopp inspired hope. Following these two great signs from heaven, the total solar eclipse of February 26, 1998, signified a third sign: an inpouring of Divine Love.

Whatever you, dear reader, may think of the foregoing, it is the author's hope that it can serve as a stimulus to look at certain phenomena of the present world with new eyes. *"You shall know the truth and the truth shall make you free"* (John 8:32)—this is the uppermost concern. In the light of truth, we will be able to recognize the Antichrist and his prophet. And it will be possible to find the Etheric Christ. The present 3 1/2 years of renewed activity of the Etheric Christ—culminating in September 1999—are "years of grace" on the positive sides of evolution, balancing out the 3 1/2 years of Antichrist that are to come. We may think in this connection, by way of analogy, of the *"seven years of plenty"* and the *"seven lean years"* of the patriarch Joseph in the Old Testament (Gen. 41:1-44). Now is the time to attune to the Etheric Christ, especially in view of the "moral eclipse" that will overtake the world through the influence of the prince of darkness. And one very important moment in time for the attunement to the Etheric Christ will be during the months after the September 1999 [Grail] Christ event, especially at the transition from 1999 to 2000. At this point in time—on January 1, 2000—the Sun will return to 16° Sagittarius (sidereal), where it was at the birth of Jesus in Bethlehem, returning to its zodiacal birthplace for the 2000th time.[41] The 2000th anniversary of the birth of Jesus will be a hidden cause for jubilation on the first day of the new millennium (hidden from most people). May this event be celebrated in its true significance, even if by only a relatively small number of people! Jesus Christ himself will respond to each one who acknowledges him!

For the event on January 1, 2000, is to the approaching etheric Golgotha event—September 3-5, 1999—as Pentecost was to the Mystery of Golgotha. At that time 50 days (actually 49 days) lay between the two events, which were events on the physical plane of existence. Now, at the end of the millennium, the two events—taking place in the etheric realm—are separated by 118 days, which is 4 x 29 1/2 days, i.e., four lunar synodic periods. (The synodic period of the Moon is the time between New Moon and New Moon, or Full Moon and Full Moon, on average 29 1/2 days.) For events taking place in the etheric, the lunar synodic period is of key significance, as the Moon indicates the boundary of the Earth's etheric body.

The period of four lunar synodic months can be thought of as indicating stages of resonance from the prime up to the octave, each half lunar month. The Golgotha event in the etheric is mirrored back to itself (prime interval) after half a lunar month, and then again (second) after a further half lunar month, to sound back as an octave of itself on January 1, 2000, whereby each New Moon and Full Moon during this period—up to the New Moon on January 6, 2000—is significant.

The "World Pentecost" on January 1, 2000, will be the octave of the Golgotha event in the etheric taking place September 3-5, 1999. And just as the Etheric Christ is central to this Golgotha event, so is Divine Sophia at the center of the approaching World Pentecost. She is seeking to bring about the birth of Christ within, to transform human beings from disciples into apostles. This is the significance of the event at the start of the

"Sophianic Millennium," signifying the start of a new era for all human beings (who consciously choose this) in their relationship to Christ and Sophia.

At the turn of the millennium the Sun returns for the 2000th time to 16° sidereal Sagittarius, where it was located at the birth in Bethlehem two thousand years ago. And the Moon at 12° sidereal Libra is opposite its position at the birth in Bethlehem, when it was at 12° sidereal Aries. Thereby it is in conjunction (at 13° sidereal Libra) with its position at the crucifixion on Golgotha.[42] This heavenly configuration at the start of the new millennium signifies a birth and a death—the birth of a new era, that of Sophianic Christianity, and the death of an old era. In truth, metamorphosis is perhaps a better word here than either birth or death, signifying the transformation from the old to the new. And these spiritual cosmic events are not of a transitory nature. Rather, they are lasting, serving as Foundation Stones for the spiritual life of the new millennium. May we all be inspired to celebrate these great events at the end of the millennium in a worthy way, to help the new come to birth within—and also without—for the creation of a new humanity and a new culture.

Conclusion

To conclude this book and this chapter about the great signs from heaven, it is appropriate also to mention the conjunction of Jupiter and Saturn at the end of May in the year 2000. Already at the time of the Christ event during the first week of September 1999 (Mystery of Golgotha in the etheric), Jupiter (10° Aries) and Saturn (22° Aries) will be close to one another (just 12° apart) in sidereal Aries, intensifying the Golgotha mood, bearing in mind that at the original Mystery of Golgotha the Sun was in the middle of sidereal Aries. In early September 1999 there will undoubtedly be a Golgotha mood encompassing the whole world.

Moreover, at the time of crossing the threshold into the new millennium on January 1, 2000, there could be a major crisis on account of the computer "millennium bug."[43] And it is reasonable to assume that the effects of this crisis already will have begun to make themselves felt by September 1999 and will probably continue for the first six to eight weeks of the year 2000 (as a realistic estimate of the impact of this problem). In this connection the following words of Rudolf Steiner are relevant:

> As the year 1000 was approaching, human beings in Europe lived in fear and expectation of the end of the world, which was awaited in a physical sense as a dissolution of the Earth in smoke and mist. It was Ahrimanic spirits who brought this idea to human beings, that something terrible would take place on the physical plane, whereas in reality much was taking place in the spiritual world. At the close of each millennium, the Ahrimanic and Luciferic spirits have special power. . . . It is these Ahrimanic spirits which are again making their influence felt as we approach the year 2000.[44]

The main weapon of the Ahrimanic (Satanic) spirits is fear, and in the year 1999—in view of the Christ event in the etheric world taking place then on September 3-5—we can expect increasing fear to be a powerful counterforce. Fear has the effect of causing contraction of the etheric body. Fear will serve to counter the expansion of the etheric body into the etheric world, an expansion that is needed in order to connect with the coming Christ event—which, in Rudolf Steiner's words quoted earlier, "will have as fundamental significance for the evolution of humanity as the event of Palestine had at the beginning of our era." The greatest event in human history since the Mystery of Golgotha is approaching. Simultaneously, every effort will be made to distract humanity from this event, particularly through inspiring fear about the future.

This does not mean that there will not be real problems. Mentioned above is the problem of an obviously Ahrimanic nature that is already causing concern about the future: the "millennium bug" that is beginning to affect many computer-operated systems. The problem—also known as the Y2K problem—is the result of computer programs having been written utilizing an abbreviated date. In such cases, dates since the year 1900 have been written in abbreviated form, leaving out the "19." This is fine for dates in the twentieth century, but clearly it will not work when the date January 1, 2000, becomes abbreviated 01.01.00. This date and all subsequent dates present a problem in the case of software comprising computer programs utilizing abbreviated dates. On a purely rational level, any problem of a mechanical nature should be able to be solved, given time, resources, and expertise. The millennium bug is a complex problem, which is being worked upon, but it is a question as to how many computer-operated systems will be able to handle dates from January 1, 2000 onwards, not to mention what will happen to some of the billions of computer chips (those that are date-sensitive) embedded in electrical utilities, satellites, airplanes, and air traffic control systems around the world.[45]

Clearly, the worst thing that could happen would be if people were to panic, fearing a widespread collapse of normal facilities that are computer-dependent. Panic, arising through mounting fear, is an unknown factor as the new millennium approaches. If no one panics, and everyone remains calm, this computer problem can surely be dealt with (and the same applies to every other problem or crisis situation), even if it will take time and might cause some degree of inconvenience before it is rectified.

On the human side, not to fear and not to panic is a sign of inner strength—strength which comes from inner security and trust in the future, regardless of outer circumstances: essentially trust in oneself as a spiritual being with a destiny and a task to fulfill in relation to humanity and the Earth. Furthermore, any problem or crisis can present an opportunity for people to unite together in a common endeavor to help one another and society at large, which is a constructive manner of facing the challenges that any disruption of normal facilities might entail. Over and above this, however, it will be of the utmost importance not to lose sight—in the face of whatever challenges may arise—of the spiritual events taking place connected with the Christ and with Divine Sophia. For it is precisely through being spiritually attuned that, ultimately, the right course of action in any given situation can be found. And through spiritual attunement to the approaching Christ event (Etheric Golgotha) and the following Sophia event (World Pentecost), a powerful source of help and inspiration will become available to anyone who is able to open up to it.

As an example of the need to remain attuned to higher spiritual reality even during a time of crisis, let us return to consider the problem of the millennium bug (Y2K). Moreover, let us recall Rudolf Steiner's words spoken in relation to the year 1000, and let us suppose that they probably pertain also to the year 2000. "It was the Ahrimanic spirits who brought this idea to human beings, that something terrible would take place on the physical plane, whereas in reality much was taking place in the spiritual world." In other words, in relating this quote to January 1, 2000, it would now read: "It is the Ahrimanic spirits who are bringing this idea to human beings, that something terrible is to take place on the physical plane, whereas in reality much is taking place in the spiritual world." If we accept that the computer is largely Ahriman's domain, then clearly the Y2K problem has very much to do with the Ahrimanic spirits. This problem will become actual on January 1, 2000. Already it is drawing a lot of energy and attention. And major disruptions could arise because of it. However, as referred to already, the extraordinary fact is that January 1, 2000, is the date of the 2000th return of the Sun to its position in the sidereal zodiac at the birth of Jesus. Thus we can truly say of January 1, 2000, that "in reality much is taking place in the spiritual world."

The date of birth of Jesus of Nazareth was shortly before midnight on December 6, 2 B.C.[46] So the date December 6, 1999, falls exactly two thousand years later (remembering that 2 B.C. is the year -1 astronomically). In terms of historical dates, therefore, the 2000th anniversary of the date of Jesus' birth falls on December 6, 1999. However, the true significance of celebrating one's birthday is that on this day the Sun, which takes one year to orbit the zodiac, returns to the same position in the zodiac where it was at birth. At the time of Jesus' birth, the Sun was at 16° Sagittarius in the sidereal zodiac, that is, almost exactly in the middle of the constellation of the Archer.[47]

Owing to the precession of the equinoxes, whereby the vernal point shifts backwards through the constellations at a rate of one degree every 72 years, the date upon which the Sun returns to the same part of the zodiacal constellation shifts backwards gradually during the course of centuries. This is because our calendar is determined in relation to the Sun's orbit in such a way that the Sun's location at the vernal point occurs on or around March 21 each year. Another thing that has to be taken into consideration is that whereas at the time of Christ the Julian calendar was in use in the Roman empire, now we use the Gregorian calendar. Making allowance for the change of calendar and for the precession of the equinoxes, the Sun returns now, in our time, to the middle of the constellation of the Archer around January 1 each year. Thus, it will be at 16° Sagittarius, where it was at the birth of Jesus, on January 1/2, 2000. This will be its 2000th return to this position. This event is surely worthy of celebration. What a difference it would make to the beginning of the new millennium if this 2000th anniversary could be widely celebrated! What a different perspective this offers for the future: the beginning of an era of Cosmic Christianity! And what strength could be drawn from a conscious celebration of this event at the start of the new millennium!

Given the mood of crisis that might prevail at the turn of the millennium on account of the Y2K problem, it may be difficult for people to focus upon the higher spiritual significance of celebrating January 1, 2000, as the 2000th birthday commemoration (in a cosmic sense) of the birth of Jesus of Nazareth, in which case it will not be easy for the

Pentecostal mood, referred to above, to break through. At this time Jupiter (0 1/2° Aries) and Saturn (15 1/2° Aries) will be just 15° apart in sidereal Aries. Thereafter Jupiter and Saturn will draw ever closer to one another, until Jupiter enters into conjunction with Saturn at the tail end of the Ram (28° Aries) on May 28/29, 2000, just two weeks prior to Pentecost, which falls on June 11 in the year 2000.

By the time of the conjunction between Jupiter and Saturn at the end of May 2000, it could well be that the Pentecost mood will really be able to break through, if the problems connected with Y2K have been largely resolved by then. Furthermore, the conjunction between Jupiter and Saturn in Aries will signify the birth of something new, given that Aries, as the first sign of the zodiac, generally denotes the start of a new cycle. At the same time, it would appear that this conjunction of Jupiter and Saturn will be a primary cosmic indicator for the new impulse streaming in, the seed of which will have been sown by the Christ event occuring nine months earlier (around September 3-5, 1999). Here we have the image of conception (Etheric Golgotha) followed by birth (World Pentecost) nine months later. Against this background it is possible to imagine that the Pentecost mood will most likely be borne by a new optimism that should begin to prevail by May 2000, enhanced and heightened by the occurence of the Jupiter-Saturn conjunction. In this respect, the end of May/beginning of June in the year 2000, leading up to Pentecost Sunday on June 11, will surely be a decisive time of fruition for the new impulse sown nine months earlier in 1999. And we may anticipate that this flowering may continue on at least until the heliocentric conjunction of Jupiter and Saturn takes place between midsummer and the festival of St. John the Baptist on June 24, 2000. (The heliocentric conjunction of Jupiter and Saturn occurs at 27 1/4° sidereal Aries on June 22/23, following the summer solstice on June 20/21.) The geocentric conjunction of Jupiter and Saturn toward the end of May, the festival of Pentecost two weeks later, and the heliocentric conjunction of Jupiter and Saturn just after the summer solstice together provide a focus for the Sophia Mystery (World Pentecost) following in the wake of the Christ Mystery (Etheric Golgotha) nine months earlier. This Sophia Mystery—also deeply connected with the 2000th celebration of the birth of Jesus on January 1, 2000—will signify a foundation stone for the Sophianic

Christianity of the future characterizing the "Sophianic Millennium" beginning in the year 2000. Thus the conjunction of Jupiter and Saturn at the tail end of sidereal Aries in the year 2000 belongs to the "great signs from heaven" denoting the beginning—in a cosmic sense—of the new millennium.

Endnotes

1. Robert A. Powell, *Chronicle of the Living Christ: Foundations of Cosmic Christianity* (Hudson, N.Y.: Anthroposphic Press, 1996) (hereafter cited as *Chronicle*).
2. Rudolf Steiner spoke of the New Age, the "Age of Light,"as having begun in the year 1899. Since the year 1899 denotes the start of the first 33 1/3-year period of the twentieth century, which culminated with the entrance of Christ into the Earth's etheric aura one-third of the way through this century, it is certainly true to regard 1899 as the cosmically initiated commencement of the New Age. From an earthly standpoint, however, the end of the first 33 1/3-year period after this cosmic commencement signified the onset of the Second Coming—and therewith the start of the New Age—for the Earth and humankind. The period between 1899 and 1933 was a time of integration of Christ's etheric body into the Earth's etheric aura.
3. The zodiac used in hermetic astrology is the *sidereal zodiac,* which was originally defined by the Babylonians and was used by them from the fifth century B.C. onward as an astronomical frame of reference and for casting horoscopes. This zodiac became transmitted to Egypt and was also used by Greek astrologers. It even became transmitted to India, where it is still used to this day by Indian astrologers, albeit with minor modifications. Two ephemerides listing daily positions of the Sun, Moon, and planets in the sidereal zodiac has been compiled by Neil Michelsen and published by Astro Computing Services (*The American Sidereal Ephemeris, 1976-2000,* San Diego, 1981 and *2001-2025,* San Diego, 1995). Cf. Robert Powell and Peter Treadgold, *The Sidereal Zodiac* (AFA Publications, Tempe, 1985) and Robert Powell, *The Zodiac: A Historical Survey* (ACS Publications, San Diego, 1984).
4. Powell, *Chronicle,* 415.
5. Rudolf Steiner, *The Evolution of Consciousness,* trans. C. Davy (London: Rudolf Steiner Press, 1966), 185-86.
6. Rudolf Steiner, *At the Gates of Spiritual Science,* trans. C. Davy (London: Rudolf Steiner Press, 1970), Lecture 14 (hereafter cited as *Gates*).
7. Rudolf Steiner, *Bilder okkulter Siegel und Säulen* (Dornach, Switzerland: Rudolf Steiner Verlag, 1977), 112-13.
8. Rudolf Steiner, *The Four Seasons and the Archangels,* trans. C. Davy and D. Osmond (London: Rudolf Steiner Press, 1968), 66.
9. Johanna and Adalbert von Keyserlingk, *Koberwitz 1924* (Stuttgart: Verlag Hilfswerk Elisabeth, 1974), 75-76.
10. Further aspects of Christ's path to the Mother are described in Robert Powell's *The Most Holy Trinosophia* (Great Barrington, Mass.: Golden Stone Press, 1990). Scheduled to be republished in an expanded form by Anthroposophic Press in 1999.

11. Two further examples are Prof. Joseph Rotblat and Group Captain Leonard Cheshire, who witnessed the A-bomb explode over Nagasaki as Churchill's official observer, and later, following a Christian conversion when someone said to him "God is a person and you know it," devoted his life to providing proper homes for the disabled (there are now 265 such Cheshire Homes in 48 countries).
12. "Asclepius, Book III" in *Hermetica,* Vol. I, trans. Walter Scott (Boulder, Colo.: Shambhala Publications, 1982), 335.
13. The same cruelty is active in the Chinese annexation of Tibet, in contradistinction to the boundless compassion of the Mahayana Buddhism of the Dalai Lama and the Tibetan Buddhists.
14. Shakespeare, *The Merchant of Venice,* Act IV, Scene 1.
15. Steiner, *Gates,* 140.
16. Ibid.
17. von Keyserlingk, *Koberwitz 1924,* 76.
18. Rudolf Steiner, *Man: Hieroglyph of the Universe,* trans. G. and M. Adams (London: Rudolf Steiner Press, 1972), 167.
19. Powell, *Chronicle,* 206-207.
20. For a detailed account, see Robert Powell, *Christian Hermetic Astrology: The Star of the Magi and the Life of Christ* (Hudson, NY: Anthroposophic Press, 1998), 71-81 (hereafter cited as *Christian Hermetic Astrology*).
21. This quote has been translated by Robert Powell from Soloviev's *Gesammelte Werke* (Complete Works) in German, vol. 8, 247.
22. For the dating of the zodiacal ages on the basis of a secure definition of the sidereal zodiac, see Robert Powell, *Hermetic Astrology,* vol. I: *Astrology and Reincarnation* (Kinsau, Germany: Hermetika, 1987), chap. 3.
23. Robert Powell, *Hermetic Astrology,* vol. II: *Astrological Biography* (Kinsau, Germany: Hermetika, 1989), chap. 9.
24. Rudolf Steiner, *Zur Geschichte und aus den Inhalten der erkenntniskultischen Abteilung der Esoterischen Schule,* 1904-1914 (Dornach, Switzerland: Rudolf Steiner Verlag, 1987), 361.
25. Positions are given as computed in the *Christian Star Calendar* by Robert Powell and Michael Brinch (Vancouver, B.C.: Sun Cross Press, published yearly). See also Neil Michelsen, *The American Sidereal Ephemeris, 1976-2000* (San Diego, Calif.: Astro Communications Services, 1981).
26. See Powell, *Hermetic Astrology,* vol. II, chap. 8.
27. Rudolf Steiner, *Prayer,* trans. Gilbert Church (Hudson, N.Y.: Anthroposophic Press, 1977), 10-12.
28. Powell, *Christian Hermetic Astrology.*
29. Rudolf Steiner, *Man's Being, His Destiny and World Evolution,* trans. E. McArthur (Hudson, N.Y.: Anthroposophic Press, 1966), 9-10.
30. Powell, *Chronicle.*

31. Rudolf Steiner, *The True Nature of the Second Coming* (London: Rudolf Steiner Press, 1971).

32. Ibid. (see lecture of January 25, 1910). He also indicated the importance of the years 1935 and 1937, as well as 1933.

33. Rudolf Steiner, "Geisteswissenschaftliche Menschenkunde" (lecture of December 21, 1908; complete works, vol. 107).

34. See Powell, *Chronicle* for details concerning the 33 1/3-year rhythm of the etheric body of Jesus Christ, the last 3 1/2 years of which relate to Christ's activity in the time between the baptism in the Jordan and the Mystery of Golgotha.

35. Rudolf Steiner, *From Jesus to Christ* (London: Rudolf Steiner Press, 1973), 46. For details concerning this Christ event, see further, Robert A. Powell and Michael Brinch, *Christian Star Calendar 1998.*

36. Powell, *Chronicle,* 316-17, 490.

37. Daniel Andreev, *The Rose of the World* (Hudson, N.Y.: Lindisfarne Press, 1997), 356-57.

38. Thomas Schipflinger, *Sophia-Maria* (York Beach, Maine: Samuel Weiser, 1998).

39. Sandra L. Zimdars-Swartz, *Encountering Mary* (Princeton, N.J.: Princeton University Press, 1991).

40. Nick Begich and Jeane Manning, *Angels Don't Play This HAARP* (Anchorage: Earthpulse Press, 1996).

41. Powell, *Chronicle,* 149 (chart 4).

42. Ibid., 149 (chart 4) and 151 (chart 6).

43. See Robert Powell's essay "The Christ Event in the Year 1999 and the Start of the New Millennium," *Christian Star Calendar 1999.*

44. Rudolf Steiner, from a lecture held in Stuttgart on March 7, 1914 (quotation translated from the German by Robert Powell). This lecture was published in *Bilder okkulter Siegel und Säulen,* Complete Works, vol. 284 (Dornach, Switzerland: Rudolf Steiner Verlag, 1977).

45. For a constructive approach to the Y2K problem, see Judy Laddon, Tom Atlee, and Larry Shook, eds., *Awakening: The Upside of Y2K* (Spokane, Wash.: The Printed Word, 1998).

46. Powell, *Chronicle,* 32.

47. Ibid., 149.

For further study of specific topics:

On the relationship of the Beatitudes to the various members of the human being, see Rudolf Steiner, *The Gospel of St. Matthew*, Lecture 9. See also Valentin Tomberg, *Anthroposophical Studies of the New Testament*, Chapter 3.

Concerning dating of the Second Coming, see Robert Powell, *Hermetic Astrology* I, Appendix II ("The Second Coming"), *Hermetic Astrology* II, Chapter 9 ("The New Age and the Second Coming"), and *Chronicle of the Living Christ*, Afterword. Further aspects concerning the Second Coming are outlined in *Christian Hermetic Astrology: The Star of the Magi and the Life of Christ*, where also the 29 $^1/_2$-year rhythm in relation to communion with Christ's astral body is discussed.

For a detailed account of the life of Christ in its historical, biographical aspect, see Robert Powell's *Chronicle of the Living Christ*, in which the exact length of Christ's life from birth in Bethlehem to the moment of resurrection is shown to be 33 $^1/_3$ years less 1 $^1/_2$ days.

For a penetrating—and at the same time an artistic/dramatic—look at the message of the giant comets Hyakutake (1996) and Hale-Bopp (1997), see *Signs in the Heavens at the End of a Millennium* by Star Fire Three (David Tresemer, William Bento, Robert Schiappacasse) (Hygiene, Colo.: Sun Shine Press Publications, 1999)

Bibliography

Barfield, Owen. *Romanticism Comes of Age*. Middletown, Conn.: Wesleyan University Press, 1986.

Begich, Nick and Jeane Manning. *Angels Don't Play This HAARP.* Anchorage: Earthpulse Press, 1996.

Dixon, Jeane. *My Life and Prophecies*. New York: William Morrow and Co., 1969.

von Eschenbach, Wolfram. *Parzival*. Translated by H. Mustard and C. Passage. New York: Random House, 1961.

Hermetika. Volumes I-IV. Translated by Walter Scott. Boulder, Colo.: Shambhala Publications, 1982.

Hillerdal, Gunnar and Berndt Gustafsson. *Sie erlebten Christus*. Basel: Verlag die Pforte, 1979.

von Keyserlingk, Johanna and Adalbert. *Koberwitz 1924*. Stuttgart: Verlag Hilfswerk Elisabeth, 1974.

Michelsen, Neil. *The American Sidereal Ephemeris 1976-2000*. San Diego, Calif.: Astro Communications Services, 1981.

Powell, Robert A. *Christian Hermetic Astrology: The Star of the Magi and the Life of Christ.* Hudson, NY: Anthroposophic Press, 1998.

______. *Chronicle of the Living Christ: Foundations of Cosmic Christianity*. Hudson, N.Y.: Anthroposophic Press, 1996.

______. *Hermetic Astrology*. Vol. I, *Astrology and Reincarnation*. Kinsau, Germany: Hermetika, 1987.

______. *Hermetic Astrology*. Vol. II, *Astrological Biography*. Kinsau, Germany: Hermetika, 1989.

______. *The Most Holy Trinosophia*. Great Barrington, Mass.: Golden Stone Press, 1990. Scheduled for republication in an expanded form by Anthroposophic Press in 1999.

(Above books by R. A. Powell distributed by Anthroposophic Press, Hudson, N.Y.)

______. *The Zodiac: A Historical Survey*. San Diego, Calif.: Astro Communications Services, 1984.

Powell, Robert A. and Michael Brinch. *Christian Star Calendar*. Vancouver, B.C.: Sun Cross Press, published yearly. (Available from the Sophia Foundation of North America, P.O. Box 712, Nicasio, CA 94946, U.S.A.).

Powell, Robert A. and Peter Treadgold. *The Sidereal Zodiac*. Tempe, Ariz.: American Federation of Astrologers, 1985.

Prokofieff, Sergei O. *The Heavenly Sophia and the Being Anthroposophia*. London: Temple

Lodge, 1996.

Soloviev, Vladimir. "A Short Narrative About Antichrist." In *Vladimir Soloviev: Russian Mystic*, by Paul Marshall Allen. New York: Steinerbooks, 1978.

Spangler, David. *Revelation: Birth of a New Age*. Findhorn, Scotland: Findhorn Publications, 1974.

Steiner, Rudolf. *The Apocalypse of St. John*. Translated by M. Cotterell. London: Rudolf Steiner Press, 1958.

______. *At the Gates of Spiritual Science*. Translated by C. Davy. London: Rudolf Steiner Press, 1970.

______. *Bilder okkulter Siegel und Säulen*. Dornach, Switzerland: Rudolf Steiner Verlag, 1977.

______. *The Course of My Life*. Translated by O.D. Wannamaker. New York: Anthroposophic Press, 1951.

______. *The Evolution of Consciousness*. Translated by C. Davy. London: Rudolf Steiner Press, 1966.

______. *The Fall of the Spirits of Darkness*. Translated by Anna Meuss. Bristol: Rudolf Steiner Press, 1993.

______. *The Four Seasons and the Archangels*. Translated by C. Davy and D. Osmond. London: Rudolf Steiner Press, 1968.

______. *The Gospel of St. Matthew*. Translated by D. Osmond and M. Kirkcaldy. London: Rudolf Steiner Press, 1965.

______. *The Influences of Lucifer and Ahriman*. Translated by D.S. Osmond. Hudson, N.Y.: Anthroposophic Press, 1993.

______. *The Inner Aspect of the Social Question*. Translated by C. Davy. London: Rudolf Steiner Press, 1974.

______. *Man: Hieroglyph of the Universe*. Translated by G. and M. Adams. London: Rudolf Steiner Press, 1972.

______. *Man's Being, His Destiny, and World Evolution*. Translated by E. McArthur. Hudson, N.Y.: Anthroposophic Press, 1966.

______. *The Portal of Initiation*. Translated by A. Bittleston. Englewood, N.J.: Rudolf Steiner Publications, 1961.

______. *Prayer*. Translated by G. Church. Hudson, N.Y.: Anthroposophic Press, 1977.

______. *The True Nature of the Second Coming*. London: Rudolf Steiner Press, 1971.

Tomberg, Valentin. *Anthroposophical Studies of the New Testament*. Translated by R.H. Bruce. Spring Valley, N.Y.: Candeur Manuscripts, 1985. (Distributed by Anthroposophic Press: Hudson, N.Y.)

About the Author

Robert A. Powell was born in 1947 in Reading, England, and studied mathematics at the University of Sussex, graduating with a Master's degree. At the same time, he developed an interest in astronomy, and this, in turn, led him to explore the roots of astrology, the ancient science of the connections between the stars and human beings.

In the mid-seventies, while researching these fields at the British Museum in London, Powell discovered the Rudolf Steiner Bookshop and Library on Museum Street. From that moment on, Steiner's Anthroposophy or spiritual science became the esoteric or spiritual context in which he was to work: a path and a guide. Steiner's many works provided the epistemological, cosmological, and Christological foundations he sought to continue his work. But Steiner's influence, though essential, was not the only one in these formative years. For, through Steiner, he was led to the work of the German-born astrosophist Willi Sucher (1902-1985) and the Russian-born sophiologist, Valentin Tomberg (1900-1973).

From 1978 to 1982, Powell, while continuing his research, was in Dornach, Switzerland, at the Goetheanum, where he completed a eurythmy training. Since graduating from eurythmy school, still continuing to study, research, and lecture on themes arising from the practice of esoteric Christianity and astrology, Robert Powell has lived and worked as a eurythmist and movement therapist at the Sophia Foundation in Kinsau, Germany. Now he gives yearly intensive courses focusing on cosmic and sacred dance, while continuing to research and write, and to lecture and give workshops internationally.

The former editor of the *Mercury Star Journal*, a quarterly publication devoted to developing a new star wisdom, Robert Powell has written several books: on ASTRONOMY (*The Zodiac: A Historical Survey; The Sidereal Zodiac; History of the Planets; History of the Houses*); ASTROLOGY (*Hermetic Astrology*, Vols. I and II; and *Christian Hermetic Astrology: The Star of the Magi and the Life of Christ*); and ANTHROPOSOPHY (*Cosmic Aspects of the Foundation Stone*; and *The Most Holy Trinosophia*). He is the co-author with Michael Brinch of the yearly *Christian Star Calendar* and a regular contributor to the Swiss journal, *Novalis*. In 1995, Powell co-founded the Sophia Foundation of North America, which published his work *Divine Sophia, Holy Wisdom*. In 1996 his pioneering book *Chronicle of the Living Christ: Foundations of Cosmic Christianity*, containing ten years of research into the life of Christ, was published. And in 1997 the six-tape set *The Sophia Teachings*, recorded by Sounds True, came out. Also, his book *The Sign of the Son of Man in the Heavens: Sophia and the New Star Wisdom* recently appeared (1999).